CAMBRIDGE LIBRARY COLLECTION

Books of enduring scholarly value

Travel and Exploration

The history of travel writing dates back to the Bible, Caesar, the Vikings and the Crusaders, and its many themes include war, trade, science and recreation. Explorers from Columbus to Cook charted lands not previously visited by Western travellers, and were followed by merchants, missionaries, and colonists, who wrote accounts of their experiences. The development of steam power in the nineteenth century provided opportunities for increasing numbers of 'ordinary' people to travel further, more economically, and more safely, and resulted in great enthusiasm for travel writing among the reading public. Works included in this series range from first-hand descriptions of previously unrecorded places, to literary accounts of the strange habits of foreigners, to examples of the burgeoning numbers of guidebooks produced to satisfy the needs of a new kind of traveller - the tourist.

The Great Republic

Sir Lepel Henry Griffin (1838–1908) was a British administrator and diplomat in the Indian Civil Service. Beginning in Lahore in 1860, his career in India spanned nearly thirty years until he resigned in 1889 and began a new life in commerce and finance. In 1884 Griffin published *The Great Republic*, a stinging critique of the United States. Consisting partly of articles which had already appeared in the *Fortnightly Review*, Griffin's book was intended to warn Englishmen, particularly Liberals, of 'the political methods of America which strike me as thoroughly bad and corrupt'. His chief accusation was that the American political system had put power into the hands of the uneducated masses. He also condemned Americans' love of materialism, their 'philistinism', and the anti-English sentiment which he had encountered during his three-week stay there. Controversial in its day, his book is a fascinating document in the history of Anglo-American relations.

Cambridge University Press has long been a pioneer in the reissuing of out-of-print titles from its own backlist, producing digital reprints of books that are still sought after by scholars and students but could not be reprinted economically using traditional technology. The Cambridge Library Collection extends this activity to a wider range of books which are still of importance to researchers and professionals, either for the source material they contain, or as landmarks in the history of their academic discipline.

Drawing from the world-renowned collections in the Cambridge University Library, and guided by the advice of experts in each subject area, Cambridge University Press is using state-of-the-art scanning machines in its own Printing House to capture the content of each book selected for inclusion. The files are processed to give a consistently clear, crisp image, and the books finished to the high quality standard for which the Press is recognised around the world. The latest print-on-demand technology ensures that the books will remain available indefinitely, and that orders for single or multiple copies can quickly be supplied.

The Cambridge Library Collection will bring back to life books of enduring scholarly value (including out-of-copyright works originally issued by other publishers) across a wide range of disciplines in the humanities and social sciences and in science and technology.

The Great Republic

Lepel Henry Griffin

CAMBRIDGE UNIVERSITY PRESS

Cambridge, New York, Melbourne, Madrid, Cape Town,
Singapore, São Paolo, Delhi, Tokyo, Mexico City

Published in the United States of America by Cambridge University Press, New York

www.cambridge.org
Information on this title: www.cambridge.org/9781108032605

© in this compilation Cambridge University Press 2011

This edition first published 1884
This digitally printed version 2011

ISBN 978-1-108-03260-5 Paperback

THE GREAT REPUBLIC.

THE
GREAT REPUBLIC.

BY

SIR LEPEL HENRY GRIFFIN, K.C.S.I.

' The Commonwealth of Athens is become a forest of beasts.''
TIMON OF ATHENS.

" O Liberté ! que de crimes on commet en ton nom.''
JEANNE-MARIE ROLAND.

LONDON: CHAPMAN AND HALL,
LIMITED.

1884.

LONDON :
R. CLAY, SONS, AND TAYLOR,
BREAD STREET HILL, E.C.

PREFACE.

SOME portions of this little book have already appeared in the *Fortnightly Review*, and are here reproduced with the consent and, indeed, at the suggestion of the editor. My criticisms of various American characteristics attracted much attention in the United States, and a mass of hostile comment in the shape of verses and newspaper articles. I would, then, at the threshold of this book, hasten to assure Americans that it is written in no unfriendly spirit to them. If what I have said be distasteful to them, I am sorry for it, for I have had no intention to wound. I am writing for Englishmen and especially for English Liberals, and wish to point out for their avoidance those of the political methods of America which strike me as thoroughly bad and corrupt. It is necessary that Englishmen should understand, at the present time, the demoralisation which may fall upon a country which is so unwise as to surrender political power into the hands of the uneducated masses, and if, in pressing home this lesson, I have been compelled to speak somewhat roughly and frankly, the fault is less mine than that of the institutions I criticise.

CONTENTS.

CONTENTS.

CHAPTER VI.

CHAPTER VII.

CHAPTER VIII.

CHAPTER IX.

CHAPTER X.

CHAPTER XI.

THE GREAT REPUBLIC

CHAPTER I.

INTERNATIONAL CRITICISM.

WHETHER the discovery of America by Columbus has been of advantage or loss to the so-called civilised peoples of the Old World would form an interesting thesis for discussion. When we remember the gentle and refined races of Mexico and Peru trampled beneath the gross feet of Pizarro, Cortes, and the Inquisition ; or regard the savage picturesqueness of the Indian tribes that wandered over the North American continent, cruel, brutal, and happy, uninjured by and uninjuring Western culture, we cannot but look with some doubt and hesitation at America of to-day, the apotheosis of Philistinism, the perplexity and despair of statesmen, the Mecca to which turns every religious or social charlatan,

B

where the only god worshipped is Mammon, and the highest education is the share list; where political life, which should be the breath of the nostrils of every freeman, is shunned by an honest man as the plague; where, to enrich jobbers and monopolists and contractors, a nation has emancipated its slaves and enslaved its freemen; where the people is gorged and drunk with materialism, and where wealth has become a curse instead of a blessing.

America is the country of disillusion and disappointment, in politics, literature, culture, and art; in its scenery, its cities, and its people. With some experience of every country in the civilised world, I can think of none except Russia in which I would not prefer to reside, in which life would not be more worth living, less sordid and mean and unlovely.

In order that this opinion may not appear harsh, exaggerated, and unfriendly, it is necessary to say a few words on the subject of international criticism. There appears to exist an idea that the friendliness and indeed the amalgamation, social and political, of the two great branches of the Anglo-Saxon race are so to be desired, that all mutual criticism of politics or manners should be uniformly favourable, even though the praise be undeserved. I will leave

others to discuss whether there can be more in un-
candid criticism than loss of self-respect ; and only
inquire whether, if we are unable to say pleasant
things of America, it be not better to remain altogether silent.   I believe silence to be both harmful
and useless.   In the first place, America is not an
inert mass, devoid of attractive power.   It is, to
the last degree, energetic, dynamic, and aggressive,
while its attractive force is so felt within the orbit
of England that a large and increasing number of
politicians and publicists are looking to America
for the dawn of a new social and political millennium, and are recommending American remedies
for all our national disorders.   Each year the democratic tide rises higher and our institutions
become more Americanised ; while some English
statesmen are admittedly careless how high the
tide may rise, and what existing institutions it
may sweep away.   It is as well that Englishmen
should   understand   what   is   the   dream   of
advanced New York Republicans as represented
by the *World* :—

" *Ca ira !   Écrasez les infames ! !*
" The storm of revolution is looming and lowering over
Europe which will crush out and obliterate for ever the hydra-
headed monarchies and nobilities of the Old World.   In
Russia the Nihilist is astir.   In France the Communist is the
coming man.   In Germany the Social Democrat will soon

rise again in his millions as in the days of Ferdinand Lassalle. In Italy the Internationalist is frequently heard from. In Spain the marks of the Black Hand have been visible on many an occasion. In Ireland the Fenian and Avenger terrorise, and in England the Land League is growing. All cry aloud for the blue blood of the monarch and the aristocrat. They wish to see it pouring again on the scaffold. Will it be by the guillotine that cut off the head of Louis XVI.? Or by the headsman's axe that decapitated Charles I.? Cr by the dynamite that searched out the vitals of Alexander the Second? Or will it be by the hangman's noose around the neck of the next British monarch?

" No one can tell but that the coming English *sans-culottes*, the descendants of Wamba the Fool and Gurth the Swineherd, will discover the necessary method and relentlessly employ it. They will make the nobles—who fatten and luxuriate in the castles and abbeys and on the lands stolen from the Saxon, sacrilegiously robbed from the Catholic Church and kept from the peasantry of the villages and the labourer of the towns— wish they had never been born. They will be the executioners of the fate so justly merited by the aristocratic criminals of the past and the present. The cry that theirs is blue blood and that they are the privileged caste will not avail the men and women of rank when the English Republic is born. They will have to expiate their tyrannies, their murders, their lusts, and their crimes in accordance with the law given on Sinai amid the thunders of heaven : ' The sins of the fathers shall be visited upon the children even unto the third and fourth generations.' " [1]

Even if such ravings as these are dismissed as unworthy of notice, it is not the less certain that the most amiable and intelligent Americans are

---

[1] It is necessary to note that the *New York World* is edited by a German.

looking forward to a near future in which the Republican lion, having digested the aristocratic lamb, shall lie down in dignified repose with no one to question his claim to be the first of created beings in a renewed world, the secret of which he pretends to be equality applied to all except himself. For an illustration of this, it is sufficient to refer to one of the latest and most pleasing American books, entitled, *An American Four-in-Hand in Britain*, by Mr. Andrew Carnegie, which describes, with great vivacity, how a party of simple and impressionable Republicans chartered a coach at Brighton and were driven, to their immense satisfaction, through England and Scotland. Throughout this book, which is by a friendly hand, and treats British weaknesses with kindly compassion, runs the strong stream of belief in the triumph of Republicanism in England, and its regeneration "under the purifying influences of equality," which Mr. Carnegie declares is the panacea of all disorders, even a constitutional monarchy. If he would only visit Boss Kelly, surrounded by the gang of Irish thieves who rule and rob New York, and explain to them that he was in every sense their equal, I cannot but think that, during his hurried exit from the presence of the municipal

gods, he would modify his somewhat simple
political beliefs.[1]

If, then, there be those, like myself, who believe
that no greater curse could befall England than for
her to borrow political methods, dogmas and institutions from America, there seems every reason
why such should explain the grounds, good or bad,
for their belief, with which American travel may
have furnished them. The good in American
institutions is of English origin and descent ; what
is bad is indigenous, and this she now desires to
teach us. But Britannia, who, since her daughter
has become independent and carried her affections
elsewhere, has escaped the dreary *rôle* of chaperone,
may surely refuse invitations to see Columbia dance,
in fancy dress, to the tune of Yankee Doodle, and
may plead her age and figure when asked to learn
the new step. There are doubtless in English
politics and society many evils and anomalies—
privileges which cannot be defended, wrongs and
injustice and misery which must be redressed and
relieved ; but, nevertheless, the English constitution, with its ordered and balanced society from
the throne to the cottage, is the symbol and

---

[1] Mr. Andrew Carnegie, though he plumes his republican
feathers with so much complacency, is, in reality, a Scotchman
who still remains a subject of the Queen.

expression of liberty in the world. Republican institutions have had a trial for a hundred years, and, so far as outsiders can judge, their failure is complete. France under a Republic has become a by-word in Europe for weakness and truculence abroad, and financial imbecility and corruption at home ; while America, which boasts of equality and freedom, does not understand that, with the single exception of Russia, there is no country where private right and public interests are more systematically outraged than in the United States. The ideal aristocracy, or government of the best, has in America been degraded into an actual government of the worst, in which the educated, the cultured, the honest, and even the wealthy, weigh as nothing in the balance against the scum of Europe which the Atlantic has washed up on the shores of the New World.

International social criticism, which rests on a basis altogether different from political, is very apt, between England and America, to be prejudiced and unjust. Both races are strangely provincial for people who travel so much, and create grievances out of mere differences in habits and manners, while they are so near of kin as to be acutely sensibly of departures from their own standard of taste or morals. English travellers are apt to expect too much ; and men who travel uncomplainingly in Spain, where night is chiefly distinguished from day by its change of annoyance, or in Bulgaria, where the only procurable bath is a stable bucket, complain bitterly at not finding in the rude hostelries of the Western States of America the conveniences and the *cuisine* of Bignon or the Bristol. But, apart from unreasonable claims, which, throughout life, make up so large a part of our unhappiness, there exists a fruitful source of irritation to Englishmen travelling in America in the depreciatory attitude to all things English that is taken by the vast majority of Americans. It is a new and doubtless a wholesome experience for Englishmen, for on the continent of Europe, however much we may be disliked, we are regarded with a hostile respect and consideration which are flattering to the national vanity. Our habits and prejudices are indulged and consulted. The splendid hotels of the Rhine, of Switzerland and Italy were built for English travellers and in deference to English tastes and requirements, although of late years our American cousins have shared with us the venal attention of Continental landlords. But in America all this is changed. English tourists are few in number, and are lost in the vast society of travelling Americans.

Their habits, when they differ from those of the natives, are considered antiquated or objectionable ; and every American usage or institution is held up to admiration, not only as good in itself, but as better than anything to be found in " the old country." The stranger would be far more disposed to accord an ungrudging admiration to the many improvements and conveniences which America has introduced into common life, if it were not demanded so peremptorily with regard to numerous matters on which there may be a reasonable difference of opinion, or on which impartial observers would give the preference to English methods.   But whether it be hotels or railway cars, horses or carriage-building, banks or beautiful women, oysters or engineering, the ordinary American loudly asserts his superiority over England, and treats an Englishman as an imbecile creature to whom he was deigning to expound the elementary principles of social and political life. *Mr. Washington Adams in England*, a novel by Mr. R. G. White, amusingly reviewed last October in the *Saturday Review*, is as good an illustration as could be found of the worst type of American critic—ignorant and presumptuous—who, from the internal evidence of his book, could never have crossed the ocean,

discussing English life and manners. It is some
consolation to find that Mr. White does not reserve
his thunders for a subject of which he knows
nothing, and that to the September number of
The North American Review he has contributed
an article on "Class Distinctions in the United
States," which, for fierce and contemptuous abuse
of the mushroom millionaires whose evil example
is demoralising American society, exceeds anything which a partially-informed Englishman could
fairly or with propriety write. I do not, however,
desire, by criticising American society further than
it influences political and national life, to lay
myself open to the charges of bad taste or super-
ficiality which may justly be brought against Mr.
White ; and my friends in New York, Washington,
Philadelphia, and the West, whose kindness and
hospitality will always be remembered, would,
I am sure, be included by Mr. Matthew Arnold
in "the remnant" upon which he was inaudibly
eloquent in his first New York lecture—the salt
which is to purify American society, the examples
of sweetness and light which are to illumine and
beautify the degenerate western world. But
whether writers like Mr. White misunderstand
and misrepresent English society, or whether we
are as black as we are painted, British equanimity

will probably remain unshaken.[1] In either case
it is certain that the English are not popular in
the United States, although there is a far more
friendly feeling between the two nations than
existed some years ago. This is most evident
in the eastern towns, such as Boston and New
York, where the imitation of English manners
and amusements has become for the time the
fashion. Horse-racing has grown to large pro-

---

[1] In justice to Mr. Richard Grant White and in accordance with
what I understand to be his wish, the following correspondence is
published :—

330, EAST SEVENTEENTH STREET, NEW YORK,
5th March, 1884.

SIR,—Although I had seen some references to your article, " A
Visit to Philistia," I read it only the day before yesterday. With
some of your judgments I am sure that many of us here would
heartily agree—indeed have already expressed the same opinion
ourselves. As to some others, we should probably say that an acquaintance with society here would probably change them entirely
or modify them greatly. I write, however, not to trouble you with
my appreciation of your article but because in it you have mentioned
me. So far as your opinion of me or anything that I have ever done
goes, I have of course nothing to say—no right to say anything, and
I beg leave to add no desire. But I was greatly surprised to find you
speaking of me as one who had been guilty (in *Mr. Washington
Adams*) of the literary crime of discussing English life although I
had never crossed the ocean, and again as writing on a subject (the
same) of which I "knew nothing."

My surprise had two causes. The first was that in the little
"skit" in question there was no discussion of English life—none
whatever ; all discussion in it having been strictly confined to affairs
and society in this country. The other you will best gather from the
printed slip which I have obtained from my publisher, and which I

portions, fox-hunting, lawn-tennis, and cricket, are
making slow progress, and the New York dude
might almost compare, for fatuous imbecility, with
the London masher.   So far and low have English
fashions penetrated, that Mr. Stokes, the affable
proprietor of the Hoffman House, keeps no waiters
in his employ who will not consent to shave their
moustaches and cut their whiskers *à l'Anglaise.*
But in the Central and Western States, with the

inclose.   Please do me the favour to read the first page and a half
of it.

You will observe that the occasion of my letter is a matter of fact ;
as to which, however, I only point out that you have erroneously
placed me before the readers of the *Fortnightly* in the position of
a man who has presumed to write in absolute ignorance of a subject
on which the truth is that he had thoroughly informed himself,
according to the best evidence, to some purpose.

I willingly leave it to your candour and right feeling to decide
what, under the circumstances, is due either to yourself or to

Yours very respectfully,

RICHD. GRANT WHITE.

To Sir Lepel Griffin, K.C.S.I.

53A, Pall Mall,
17th April, 1884.

Sir,—In reply to your polite letter inclosing printed "opinions of
the press " on your work, *England Without and Within,* I can
only assure you that I am exceedingly sorry to have unintentionally
misrepresented you, and to have placed you in a false position before
the readers of the *Fortnightly Review.*   So far as I can correct the
mistake, by the publication of your letter, it shall be done.

I would, however, suggest that your objection to my criticism is
itself mistaken.   I did not say that you had never crossed the ocean,
but that it could not have been inferred from the internal evidence of

exception of Colorado, which is being largely developed by English settlers and capital, there is little love for England or English ways, and criticism is almost uniformly unfriendly. As an example of this may be mentioned the savage abuse of Western journals, among which raged an epidemic of discourtesy directed against some members of Mr. Villard's North Pacific party for a misapprehension, amply apologised for, which in

your book. Since receipt of your letter, I have again read *Mr. Washington Adams*, and I am unable to accept your description of it. I consider it, and the *Saturday Review* considered it, a description and discussion of English life and manners ; the scene passes in English country houses, and among persons who are by position English ladies and gentlemen, and I can only repeat that, from the internal evidence of your work, I could never have imagined you had been in England. I have never met English ladies and gentlemen such as you describe, and have no desire to do so. But I readily accept your assurance that you have deeply studied English society, and can only regret that your labours have not been more productive. I further admit that we have little of which to complain in your description of us : for I do not consider Lord Toppingham or Lady Boreham more offensive caricatures of English people than is the vulgar, aggressive prig, Mr. Mansfield Humphreys of the well-mannered, courteous American gentleman who is fully as popular in England as in his own country.

Lastly, I would observe that the newspaper *critiques* with which you have favoured me would have been of more weight had they been concerned with the book I had discussed instead of another to which I had not alluded, and which, unfortunately, I have never read.

Yours faithfully,

LEPEL GRIFFIN.

To RICHARD GRANT WHITE, ESQ.

England, and affecting American guests, would
have remained unnoticed. Americans will often
say that the sentiment of the country cannot fairly
be ascertained from newspapers ; but in a country
where the press has attained an unprecedented
development, and where newspapers are, to all
appearance, the only literature of the vast majority,
a foreigner must assume that they represent, with
some exactness, the popular opinion.   There is
no reason why the English should be popular
in America.   They are almost the most disagreeable race extant, and are often unendurable to
each other ; nor is there any part of Europe,
except perhaps Hungary, where they are not more
disliked than in the United States.   The opinion
expressed by the most original of living American
poets, the present Minister to the Court of St.
James's, represents that of most foreigners, and
it is difficult to see that it is essentially unfair :—

> " Of all the sarse that I can call to mind
> England *doos* make the most onpleasant kind :
> It's you're the sinner ollers, she's the saint :
> Wat's good's all English, all that isn't ain't.
> —She's praised herself ontil she fairly thinks
> There ain't no light in Natur' when she winks."

Such characteristics are not amiable, and the
laws of heredity have transmitted them to our

Transatlantic cousins.   It is, indeed, probable that the Americans are, intrinsically, as disagreeable as ourselves ; for although, on the continent of Europe, they are comparatively popular, this is probably because they are less known.   Annually, a flight of pork-packers and successful tradesmen cross the Atlantic, with their families, to complete an education, which has in reality not begun, by a contemplation of Paris hotels and Rhine steam-boats.   But the American pork merchant is silent in the presence of his peacock-voiced wife and daughters ; and the complete party, Philistine though it be, is infinitely preferable to the swarm of London shop-boys with their sweethearts, whose uproarious felicity makes hideous all foreign re-sorts in the near neighbourhood of England.   In the continental dislike of England is an element of jealousy and suspicion in which America has no part.   We have fought and bullied in every quarter of the world, and, to-day, we stand with crossed swords with Russia in Central Asia and Armenia, with France in China and Egypt.   Eight hundred years of victory—for the English never own a defeat —has left much soreness on every side, while the too fortunate Yankee, navyless and armyless, is not regarded, in a city like Paris, as a past or future enemy, but merely as the welcome victim of

hungry shopkcepers.   If America were as closely
connected with Europe as is England, her citizens
would be as much disliked as Englishmen.   The
two nations, however diverse their special characteristics may appear to a superficial observer, are
curiously alike. The true Americans are unaffected
by the stream of German or Scandinavian or Irish
emigration, with which they have never mingled.
They are now, and will remain, Englishmen in
thought, genius and weaknesses— the physical type
modified by an uncongenial climate mostly in
extremes, the commercial spirit intensified by
unrivalled opportunities for its successful employment, and the national genius for mechanical
invention developed by the high wages of labour,
precisely as the monkey developed a prehensile
tail.

CHAPTER II.

THE BIG THINGS OF AMERICA.

AN English characteristic, strongly developed and even grotesquely caricatured in America, is the love of big things, which is, after all, a failing akin to virtue, and which will guide America into fair pastures when adversity and Mr. Matthew Arnold shall have chastened and purified Philistia. At present, Americans are satisfied with things because they are large ; and if not large, they must have cost a great deal of money. One evening, at the Madison Square Theatre, an American observed to me, " That is the most expensive drop-scene in the world." It was a glorified curtain of embroidery, with a golden crane and a fairy landscape, and might justly have been claimed as the most beautiful drop-scene in the world ; but this was not the primary idea in the Yankee mind. The two houses most beautiful architecturally in

C

the Michigan Avenue at Chicago were shown to
me as half-a-million-dollar houses.   A horse is not
praised for his points, but as having cost so many
thousand dollars; a man, who certainly may
possess no other virtue, as owning so many
millions.   The habit of making size a reason for
admiration is less jarring to an educated taste than
that of making money the standard of beauty and
virtue.

Full in front of the White House at Washington,
as a warning to all future Presidents to avoid the
penalties which attach to patriotism, a column
of white marble is slowly rising to the memory of
Washington.   It is intended eventually to appear
as an obelisk of six hundred feet, "the highest
structure ever raised by man, excepting the Tower
of Babel."   Whether the design, which would seem
to have been framed in the spirit which brought
confusion on the builders of its prototype, will ever
be completed it is impossible to say.   The corner-
stone was laid thirty-five years ago, and something
more than half the destined height has been already
reached.   Colonel Casey, in charge of the work,
promises its early completion; but if America
continues to depart from that standard of free and
honest administration which the high-minded,
chivalrous, and clean-handed founder of the

Republic set up, it would seem that for very shame
the monument will be left unfinished, to symbolise
as the tower of a shot manufactory or a cotton-mill,
the triumph of industrial enterprise rather than of
successful patriotism. In no case will it possess
any interest beyond its size. Many nations have
begged or stolen obelisks from Egypt to decorate,
with dubious taste, their capitals. Half-a-dozen
may be found in odd corners in Rome ; London,
and Paris, and New York have each their trophy ;
and modern imitations have been raised in
cemeteries and on battle-fields in memory of those
whom the affection of friends or the gratitude of
nations have not thought worth an original design.
But the obelisk is a monolithic feature in Egyptian
architecture proportional to and in harmony with
surrounding buildings, and never placed by itself.
On the banks of the Potomac, and to the memory
of the most distinguished American, this gigantic
obelisk, although embellished with three large
windows and a patent elevator for country visitors,
is incongruous and absurd. When the next saviour
of his country shall have liberated America from
the tyranny of rings and monopolists, as much
heavier than that of George III. as were the
scorpions of Rehoboam compared with the whips
of his father, a grateful people must logically raise

C 2

a pyramid, greater than that of Cheops, to his memory.

The Metropolitan Opera House at New York which has been opened this season, is the latest illustration of the American love of big things because they are big. This theatre is said to be the largest in the world, and was built by wealthy New Yorkers who were unable to buy boxes at the original Opera House, as their proprietors did not think fit to die or vacate as quickly as the aspirants made money. The result has been the present house, in which may be nightly seen the miserable and unmusical millionaires, from Vanderbilt, like royalty, in the centre, to Jay Gould in the depth of his stage-box, like a financial spider waiting to suck the blood of a new victim, feigning a pleasure they do not feel, applauding, with consistent ignorance, at the wrong time and in the wrong place. A similar scene of anguish was surveyed by Satan when, in Milton's song, he rose from the fiery marl and addressed his peers. The new house cannot be compared with those of Paris, Vienna, Moscow, and London, which have all and each their special charm. Its architect visited Europe, and carefully collected for reproduction everything that he could find ugly or inconvenient, and then built the largest, the meanest, the most

ill-arranged opera-house, the worst for sight and
sound, to be found in the world. New York,
whose opera-going society is hardly a twentieth of
that of London in the season, cannot support two
opera-houses ; and on the six or seven occasions
that I have been in the new house it was half
empty. But the love of big things has been
gratified, although the interests of music and the
public have been sacrificed.

If a stranger were to ask an intelligent and well-
informed American what, in his opinion, was the
thing best worth seeing in the United States, he
would probably name the pork-packing establishments at Chicago. To this loathsome favour, like
Yorick's skull, all must come. The young beauty
on her honeymoon tour ; the statesman, the
tourist, all are drawn by some mysterious fascination to the shambles. They watch the unfortunate
swine hurry up the broad way which leads to destruction ; in absorbed horror, they see the throats
of the victims cut, and the descent of the body,
living or dead, it matters little, into the boiling
sea below, the scraping, the disembowelling and all
the revolting details of the toilette of the dead.
Few are permitted to escape the spectacle. Lord
Coleridge, carried to the shambles by his friends of
the Chicago bar, after having witnessed a few

executions, begged to be allowed to retire, as otherwise he would be unable to eat sausages again.
Whether Matthew Arnold saw and reflected on
the mystery I know not, but we will hope that the
apostle of culture refused to follow this worse than
Ashantee custom. When I declined absolutely to
witness the pig-killing, my Chicago acquaintances
were distinctly ruffled. It was hardly to be en-
dured that a mere tourist, filled with the idle
sentiment of Europe, should despise the institution
which had done most to make their city famous.
But I was firm. I respectfully pointed out that
among the evil qualities which I had inherited or
acquired, a love of seeing pigs killed was not included ; that if I were possessed of this unamiable
monomania I could gratify it in Europe, and that
I would cheerfully pay fifty dollars to avoid the
sight. I was reluctantly excused. But I foresee
that generations of tourists yet unborn will be less
fortunate ; and the pork-packing establishments of
Chicago will continue the cynosure of a nation's
eyes, ranking with the Abbey of Westminster,
the Parthenon of Athens and the Duomo of
Milan.

The only sight which, in American eyes, disputes
the pre-eminence of the Chicago slaughter-yards
is Niagara, and there may be some who would

unhesitatingly assign it the palm. Its chief beauty
consists in its being the largest waterfall in the
world, with greater capacity than any other for
producing by water-power those manufactured
abominations which, as American fabrics or novel-
ties, are gradually debasing the taste of the civilised
world. Its one drawback is that the left bank of
the Niagara river being English territory and the
main body of the fall being situated therein, Americans are unable to claim a monopoly in this
natural marvel for the States. It is fortunate for
posterity that the Canadian English have control
over the finer portion of the Niagara scenery, as
this alone protects it from such ruin as vulgarity
and greed combined can bring on nature. On a
small island, midway across the American fall, the
authorities of the State of New York—whose names
I would hand down to eternal infamy were I not
convinced that, being New York officials, they are
already as infamous as it is possible for officials to
be—have permitted the erection of a paper-mill,
hideous in its architectural deformity, and blight-
ing with a curse the beauty of Niagara. It is not
possible to describe the effect that this building has
upon a sensitive visitor. The outrage on good
taste is so extreme, and the state of nervous irritation induced by the unconscious vandalism of the

American people is so acute, that I am disposed to consider a visit to Niagara a source of more pain than pleasure. This mill is the outward and visible sign, blazoned voluntarily to the world, of American Philistinism. The Boston journals may announce the advent of the millennium of good taste ; Messrs. James and Howells and White may set forth their poor platitudes to prove the cultured and refined sentiments of their countrymen ; but the Niagara paper-mill raises its tall chimney high above the everlasting roar of the torrent to give them all the lie.

Nor is this the only outrage on good taste at Niagara. The torture of the paper-mill ceases with the daylight, and its presence may be forgotten. The traveller then, in frantic search for an emotion, may hope to wander alone to the edge of the avalanche of waters, and there commune with such soul as waiters, rival touts, and coachmen may have allowed him to retain. In the solemn moonlight the wonderful pageant seems more weird and mysterious than ever. But what is this new and unknown effect of the moonbeams ? Is it—yes, it is—the coloured lime-light, red, green, and blue, thrown upon the hoary fleece of Niagara by American cockneys ! In sheer disgust and exasperation the traveller turns his back on the insult and retires sulkily to bed. I remember, some years ago, arriving at Naples in the evening with two ladies who had never seen Vesuvius, and, as the volcano was in eruption, I anticipated great pleasure in showing them the glorious spectacle. Darkness fell, and the red lines of the molten rivers of lava burnt into sight, and the sullen clouds above the crater turned to crimson. But suddenly a long line of bright points of light appeared from the observatory along the crest of the mountain. These were lamps of electric light, which the Neapolitan municipality, who would make a profit out of the Day of Judgment if it were possible, had set up to guide visitors along a wire tramway to the summit. If I remember rightly, the work was afterwards destroyed by the lava, and I sincerely trust its promoters and constructors were burnt with it. But the disgust with which I saw those electric lights degrading the most majestic of nature's phenomena to the level of Cremorne or Mabille was repeated in my heart as I looked upon the lime-lights at Niagara.

On the whole, and always excepting the Chicago pig-shambles, I am disposed to think Niagara the sight best worth seeing in America, though I will never return there until the paper-mill shall have been removed. I will not attempt to describe the indescribable, and would merely note for the benefit of future travellers that the effect of Niagara is as follows. On the first day it is distinctly disappointing : the roar of the waters is not so loud, the fall so high, or the current so fierce as was imagined. On the second day this natural though irrational disappointment has been gradually and unconsciously swallowed up by the waterfall, which has become omnipresent, tremendous, and soul-absorbing. On the third day Niagara has grown a monster so oppressive to soul and sense that the visitor hurries from the place with the feeling that another day's communing with the waters would make him mad. Such, at any rate, were my sensations, and I found them almost identical with those of my three fellow travellers.

The last, though by no means the least, annoyance connected with Niagara is the all-prevading presence of brides. When a young American's fancy lightly turns to thoughts of love, he vibrates to Niagara as the needle to the pole. Here he brings his bride for the honeymoon, whether from the facilities offered for suicide, or for other and more recondite reasons, unconnected with the beauty of the scenery, I know not ; though my belief, founded on prolonged observation, is that the choice is due to the fact

that Niagara is the place in the world where two
persons, who have nothing to say to each other,
can remain silent without embarrassment for the
longest period of time, the noise of the water
forbidding all but pantomimic conversation. However this may be, brides and bridegrooms are
everywhere to be seen, making demonstrative if
silent love under every tree and on every point
of danger overhanging the torrent. There are
perhaps earthly conditions in which the identity
of a bride may remain concealed, for other women
besides her are demonstrative in their affection
and wear new frocks. But Niagara, with its
almost perpendicular descents to the river, is
peculiarly favourable to the display of the
feminine foot and ankle ; and the bride invariably
wears new boots, which is done by no other sane
woman on a country excursion. The time to
visit Niagara is in the early spring or in the late
autumn, before the arrival, or after the departure,
of tourists, and when all hotels save one are closed.
The visitor may then, for a time, be happy,
especially if he has induced Mr. Patrick Ford,
the editor of the *Irish World,* to blow up the
paper-mill with the dynamite collected for his
scientific war with England.

In the Mississippi, the Americans may confidently

boast of possessing a river larger and longer than any to be found elsewhere. The Thames and the Tiber, the Danube and the Ganges, though not without historical interest or commercial import-ance, are pigmies beside this river giant. Yet, in beauty, the Mississippi is not to be compared with the clear St. Lawrence, or fifty smaller American streams. Indeed its waters are but liquid mud, and the scenery, in the lower part of its course, is chiefly composed of swamps and sand banks. Further to the north its beauty increases, and at St. Paul in Minnesota, two thousand miles from its mouth, the river flows between cliffs which would be imposing were it not that they are decorated with the announcement, in letters twenty feet high, that "*Smith's chewing tobacco is the best.*" At St. Louis, nearly a thousand miles nearer the sea, and after its junction with the Missouri, the river has become a superb volume of pea-soup; and thence pursues a thoroughly uninteresting and unlovely course to the sea, doing as much mis-chief as it can on the way.

The manner in which Americans permit their most beautiful scenery to be spoiled by the rapacity of vulgar advertisers, notifying their respective swindles on rocks and stones and trees, or by the erection of the most commonplace or ugly buildings in most incongruous situations, is hardly to be explained except on the supposition that the long and absorbed contemplation of the dollar has destroyed any popular appreciation of natural beauty. The question is one of great psychological interest, and some obscurity, for the deepest love of nature and the fullest delight in natural beauty fill the works of such American poets as Bryant and Longfellow, and dignify the obscene ravings of Walt Whitman. Yet on what reasonable ground can we account for the Niagara paper-mill? It is not that the love of freedom in the States is so keen that the individual right of the manufacturer to erect his building over the waterfall cannot be safely disputed. The whole argument of this book is to show that such cannot be the explanation, since individual right is not regarded in America when opposed to the wishes or prejudices of the majority, or of that minority which, by impudence and audacity, has usurped the prerogatives of the majority. Democracy is everywhere tyranny ; in the same sense and only differing in degree from that socialistic tyranny which Mr. Herbert Spenser has made the text of his latest warning. If the New York people thought the Niagara paper-mill the outrage on decency which it is, they would sweep it away without a thought of the individual rights which they well know have been acquired by bribing the State officials. It would almost seem that the sense of beauty was so faint in Americans that the desecration of beautiful scenery excited no sensation of annoyance in their minds. The elevated railway in New York is a striking example of this bluntness of æsthetic perception. To a stranger this work appears altogether fatal to the beauty of the streets. But no one has ever heard a New Yorker object to it on æsthetic grounds. On the contrary, it is considered a chief glory of the city, and a noteworthy sign of its marvellous enterprise and activity. One memorable event has occurred in modern American history which would, at first sight, appear to suggest the existence of a popular love of natural beauty. This was the Act of Congress in 1872, constituting that strange region in the northwestern part of the territory of Wyoming, which is undoubtedly one of the most remarkable and beautiful districts in the known world, a public park or pleasure-ground for the benefit and enjoyment of the people. But this action, though deserving of every commendation, is still open to criticism. The Yellowstone National Park is 3,575 square miles in extent, that is to say, the size of

Kent, Sussex, and Surrey together ; and it is obvious that as the country becomes populated, and
Wyoming passes from a wild and uninhabited
Territory to the higher political rank of an independent State, the Act of Congress will be a dead
letter.   As well attempt to hold Leviathan with a
hook as to maintain this enormous tract of country
in savage isolation.   Before many years shall have
passed the paper-maker will have his inevitable
chimneys over the Mammoth Falls, and the rocks
of the Grand Cañon will invite the traveller to
invest in Trego's Teabury Tooth Wash or Conger's
Chest Shields.   The whole transaction was a piece
of swagger which was known to be meaningless.
Probably no single member of Congress who voted
for the Bill had ever seen the Yellowstone country.
Even to this day it is not visited by Americans,
and, with the exception of the "free-lunchers"
who were drawn in Mr. Villard's ephemeral
triumph across the continent last autumn, on the
occasion of the opening of the Northern Pacific
Railway, I have never met an American who had
seen the Yellowstone Park.   Of twenty tourists
who have visited it, nineteen are Englishmen ; and
Americans will tell you that they have a great deal
too much to do to be fooling around looking after
beautiful scenery.   Saratoga and Newport are quite

distant enough for their holiday, while the more
enthusiastic will penetrate to Lakes George and
Champlain, the White Mountains and the banks of
the St. Lawrence.   In the most beautiful parts of
the Rocky Mountains, in the finest season of the
year, I do not remember to have met a single
American travelling for pleasure and enjoyment
of the scenery.

One of the most "elegant resorts" for tourists, in
the near neighbourhood of New York and Philadelphia, is Delaware Water Gap, where the Delaware
river forces its way through the Blue Mountains.
The country is richly wooded and park-like ; cata-
racts, sylvan glades, bold cliffs, and many-tinted
foliage make the scene one of enchanting and
every-varying delight.   But more remarkable than
woods or waters is the elaborate system of sign-
boards which you encounter in every direction.

To Emily's Rest, 1 Mile.   To Rebecca's Bath, ½ Mile.
Take the Right-hand Path for CHILDS'S ARBOR.

Or like this :

Keep to the Left ! !
Only 5 16 Mile Further to CHILDS'S ARBOR.

The following explanation from a local guide-
book struck me as so comical that I reproduce
it here :

" The place to which your willing feet are directed by a
score of painted clapboards and half a hundred lettered
shingles is at the brow of the hill, overlooking the river and
the gap. Through a rift or flume, a tiny stream makes its
way down in a series of cascades and pools. In among the
trees, over the running water—which at certain seasons
hardly more than drips in tear drops, while the wind sighs
through the melancholy hemlocks—there has been erected,
at the expense of Mr. G. Washington Childs, A.M., the
proprietor of the *Public Ledger* of Philadelphia, a rustic
structure accurately represented in the following picture.*

" This is Childs's Arbour. The most conspicuous feature
of the exterior is the immense monogram, G. W. C., so
placed that it can be seen from every point whence the
arbour itself is visible. For many years this has been the
favourite place for Mr. Childs's meditations. He finds
inspiration in the surroundings.

" In rustic letters, inside the obituary bower, the motto
of the Childs family is displayed :

INVENIAM VIAM AUT FACIAM.

" This is in one sense a cryptogram, since it modestly and
ingeniously conceals the honorary degree conferred upon the
poet by Princeton College. The key is as follows :

INVENI-A. M. VI-A. M. AUT FACI-A. M.
G. WASHINGTON CHILDS-A. M.

* Here, in the original, was a rough woodcut, representing the bower.

D

" Although there is a booth hard by, where lager beer and
lemonade are sold to the thirsty wayfarer, nobody ever
disturbs the poet when he is known to be in his arbour.   In
his absence, however, visitors freely enter the retreat, and
hundreds of autographs, scrawled and cut upon the graceful
structure, testify to the reverence with which the great and
good man is regarded by his fellow citizens."

Mr. George Washington Childs is probably the
only man in Philadelphia who is widely known in
England.   His honour in his own country I did
not find to be greater than that of most other
prophets; but he is doubtless a man of intelligence
and culture.   Yet since Dickens drew the picture
of Boffin's bower, no more grotesque picture has
been presented than this Philadelphian editor ad-
vertising himself in his brand-new "family" motto,
invented to modestly include his blushing College
honours; and writing fifth-rate verse in the
cockney "arbour," with beer-drinking worshippers
respectfully gazing upon the poetic frenzy of "the
great and good man" from the neighbouring booth.
Is such ridiculous posturing among the sacred
mysteries of nature compatible with that reverent
spirit which inspires nature's poet ?   Can a people
have any true perception for the beautiful, or any
deep sense of the modesty of nature who do not
overwhelm Mr. Childs and his arbour with
unextinguishable laughter !

CHAPTER III.

SCENERY AND CITIES.

I HAVE already said that America is the country of disillusion and disappointment, in politics, literature, culture, and art; in its scenery, its cities, and its people; and I would here explain the limited sense in which this criticism is intended to apply to scenery and cities. My remarks can only be general, seeing that I have no ambition to enter into competition with the guide-books, or do more than note those superficial characteristics of America which cannot fail to attract the attention of every intelligent traveller. I would then observe that to a person who has travelled much and has seen the most striking and beautiful parts of both Europe and Asia, the scenery of the United States and Canada appears singularly unattractive and tame. There is some fine scenery, but the country is so vast, and

D 2

the distances to be traversed so wearisome, that the impression made by the oases of loveliness is effaced by the monotony of the general ugliness. The prairie has been the favourite theme of poets and novelists: its illimitable extent; its carpet of flowers and its canopy of stars; its mysterious silences; its terrible awakening to life in whirlwind and fire. But the prairie of real life is a dull, uniform plain, for most part of the year burnt a dead brown; stretching in unbroken monotony for hundreds and even thousands of miles, precisely like those dismal Russian steppes across which, month after month, the poor victims of tyranny drag their failing limbs to their Siberian grave.

As the prairies are too large to be beautiful, so are the great American lakes, Superior, Michigan, and Ontario. They have much of the beauty which belongs to the sea; but on their southern shores there is little scenery of interest; and it is only where they narrow to form the St. Lawrence river, and for forty miles take the name of the Lake of the Thousand Islands, that they are in any degree noteworthy. But, although pretty, there is nothing in this renowned lake of any special beauty, and the same remark applies to the famous Lakes George and Champlain, which

American guide-books proclaim to be unequalled in the world for beauty, but which would not receive much attention were they situated in the country that owns Maggiore, Como and Garda. Such a spectacle as Lucerne on a brilliant spring morning, with Pilatus and the Righi to right and left, still covered with their crown of snow, the deep-blue lake and the multitudinous mountains in the white distance, is nowhere to be seen in the States. Of river scenery I know little, and the Hudson, the St. Lawrence, the Las Animas, Del Norte, and the Mississippi exhaust my list. The Hudson has a world-wide reputation for beauty, but strikes a European as overrated. That portion of its course in the immediate neighbourhood of New York is fine, and indeed the fifty miles to West Point is well worth seeing. After that the scenery is tame, and the beauty of the whole distance is much injured, *more Americano*, by the railway running on either bank, and cutting the river from the scenery by its level line of embankment, and by the numerous block ice houses and manufactories which occupy every specially lovely turn in the river. The St. Lawrence is, like the Mississippi or the lakes, too large to be uniformly beautiful, though it is a superb stream, and Quebec, situated at its true mouth, is from natural position incomparably the most stately and striking city that I have seen in America.   Indeed there are few cities in Europe which can match Quebec for imperial beauty.   Much of the best scenery in the States is within reasonable distance of the eastern sea board, in Pennsylvania, New York, Virginia and New Hampshire, where low ranges of picturesque mountains and an infinite variety of vegetation make in spring and autumn a veritable paradise. But, for the boldest and most characteristic scenery, it is necessary to go two thousand miles west to the Rocky Mountains, where, unless the imagination of the traveller has been unduly exalted, he will be well repaid for his labours.   The first view of the Rocky Mountains before snow has fallen on the heights, is disappointing.   They do not appear of any considerable elevation, though a few of the loftiest peaks, such as those behind Colorado Springs, are not much inferior to Mont Blanc.   This is due to the gradual rise of the prairie from the Mississippi, until at Cheyenne or Denver the traveller, though still on the open plain, is some 6,000 feet above the level of the sea.   Nor is the colouring of the mountains at all rich.   Almost devoid of vegetation on their eastern slopes, and not high enough for snow to lie throughout the year, the long range of bare, burnt hill-side rather resembles the dreary mountain ranges of Afghanistan or the Derajat than the Alps or the Pyrenees. In the spring months, before the winter snow has melted or the fierce heats of summer have baked the country to a uniform tint, the mountains are doubtless beautiful enough. So they are as I was privileged to see them, in the autumn. One day, early in October, the scene changed as if by magic: at night, no snow had been visible on the mountains, except in some few isolated patches in sheltered valleys, but heavy rain fell in the lowlands, and with the morning the Rocky Mountains were covered far down with snow. The scene then was one of surpassing beauty, and the journey from Antonito and Duvango to Silverton, the train now slowly climbing passes 11,000 feet above the sea, now winding along the bank of an impetuous river, the whole mountains from river to peak densely covered with vegetation aflame with the thousand tints with which autumn in America decorates the forest, could never be forgotten by any one who witnessed it. For the bareness of the Rocky Mountains towards the plain country in Colorado does not prepare one for the great beauty and variety of the forest when once the heart of the hills has been penetrated. One charm of railway travelling in the Rocky Mountains is due to the manner in which the lines have been constructed. In order to avoid unnecessary expenditure in this new and wild country, which, a few years ago, was almost unexplored, the line has been carried along the edge of the precipice in a thousand curves, instead of piercing the mountains by tunnels as in the St. Gothard Railway. What is thus lost in directness of route is gained in beauty of scenery. No traveller who desires to understand what America has of rich, quiet beauty, as well as of wild, savage scenery, should fail to visit some portions of the interior of the Rocky Mountains, and if his business or pleasure carries him to Salt Lake City or San Francisco, he would do well to travel by the new route through Pueblo and Gunnison, rather than by the uninteresting direct line from Cheyenne.

In speaking of the general impression left upon me by American cities, I trust that I shall not be accused of Philistinism if I give, unhesitatingly, my preference to the brand new city of Chicago, which has risen, phœnix like, from its ashes. I am well aware that many of the evils which I have hereafter described as existing in the municipal administration of New York, flourish almost as luxuriantly in Chicago. But with all its defects, upon which I do not intend to dwell, this city seems to me destined by its unrivalled position, and by the energy and public spirit of its citizens, to be the future metropolis of America. It has been planned and laid out with a noble confidence in its future. Its avenues, and magnificent series of parks surrounding the city, are not only unsurpassed but unequalled in any part of the world. It has had the good fortune to possess architects of genius, and many of the private residences are models of convenience and good taste, while the City Hall and Post Office, for beauty and dignity, might well be studied by those architects who are now submitting plans for public offices in London. Most American towns are of little interest, and their monotony, from the rectangular system on which they have been planned, is depressing to the last degree. The narrow streets, the winding ways, the perpetual surprises of unexpected views of strangeness and beauty found in the ancient cities of Europe, which have slowly grown up through a thousand years, with no definite plan, and recalling even in their inconveniences the struggles and warfare of their mediæval days, have naturally no place in American cities. The width of the streets, the admirable public buildings, and

the well built and extensive shops and places of
business, together with the general air of industry
and prosperity form their only charm, which has no
connection with the picturesque. Churches, indeed,
form an exception to the general monotony, and
to judge from their number, of every denomination,
the Americans must be, on Sundays, at any rate,
a religious people ; while there is every sign that
the Roman Catholic form of creed is gaining, in
America, all the ground that it has lost in Europe

The most noticeable defect of the towns is the
inferior character of the roadway. Paving in America seems an unknown art ; the principles of Mac-
adam have not crossed the ocean, and the paving
generally would be considered disgraceful in an
English village. Washington is, in this, as in almost
every branch of civic administration, the honourable exception, and the reason is found in the fact,
which is as significant as any in American political
life, that the district of Columbia, which is virtually
no more than the city of Washington itself, is not
delivered, like other American towns, to the tender
mercies of an inefficient and corrupt municipality.
I believe that Washington, in former days, had its
municipal troubles, and it was only bitter experience that induced it to take refuge in despotic
government from that popular administration which

Congress recommends elsewhere, but which it soon discarded when the usual results followed in the only city over which the Government of the United States can exercise any direct control.

The number of Industrial Exhibitions, both in the United States and Canada, surprises a stranger who is accustomed to the apathy of the Old World at all those times when it is not excited to international competition. Toronto, Chicago, London, St. Louis, and even Denver, with many other towns, had their exhibitions, all good, and some, especially that at Chicago, admirable. In this last was the best loan collection of pictures that I saw in America. At Denver, the Exhibition buildings had been placed too far from the town, and the show was not a financial success; but in its display of mineral wealth it was of the greatest interest. The example of America might be followed in England with great advantage to trade. In London something is being done, and the Fisheries Exhibition last year and the Sanitary Exhibition this season, together with the international show at the Crystal Palace, sufficiently testify to metropolitan public spirit. But there is no reason that the great provincial cities, like Manchester, Liverpool, Glasgow, Bristol, and Birmingham, should not annually by turns have an exhibition of arts and industries, which, with due attention to amusement, should be profitable. Industrial Exhibitions are not the most exciting form of human amusement, and it is only as a means for developing commercial enterprise that they are to be recommended. They seem to form a considerable proportion of the popular recreation in the United States, and their number and excellence are partly due to the commercial energy of the people and partly to the republican simplicity which, in a country possessing little to amuse, has adopted that form of dissipation which the jaded cities of the West have abandoned from sheer disgust and weariness of spirit. There are, however, many circles in the inferno of amusement, and it is possible to make even an Industrial Exhibition attractive, as was proved at Vienna in 1873, and by the Fisheries Exhibition in London.

CHAPTER IV.

LIBERTY.

INTERNATIONAL criticism was represented in its most attractive form by Lord Coleridge during his recent visit to the States. It is true that he was in no position to act the Mentor and unfavourably discuss American institutions. He was the guest of the American bar, and no Englishman in recent years has received in the States a more cordial or more generous welcome. The high rank and reputation of the Chief Justice, his unblemished character, and the literary distinction connected with his name, combined with his fine presence and courtly manners, impressed and charmed American society. His progress from city to city was almost triumphal, and his opinion of his hosts and their country as expressed in his speeches was doubtless heartfelt and sincere. Guests and hosts were mutually gratified. It may, however, be questioned whether it was altogether

consistent with the dignity of the Chief Justice of
England to be carried about America like Barnum's
"Greatest Show on Earth," as an advertisement
of the glory of that remarkable country. Better
the dinner of herbs with freedom, than terrapin
and canvas-back ducks with servitude. And it
must be admitted that a full expression of opinion
and indulgence of the critical or judicial spirit
were impossible in these frequent banquets and
receptions. It is not after dining with a friend
that we can best criticise the arrangement of his
house or the manners of his family. It is true
that honest criticism was neither expected nor
desired, for the Americans resemble—and herein
they are very sensible people—those authors described by Oliver W. Holmes, who, when they ask
for your criticism expect your praise, and will not
be satisfied with anything else. A Chief Justice
should only speak from the bench, where his
words carry the force and weight which is rightly
accorded to deliberate judgment, wisely formed
and temperately expressed. Not for him is the
glorious dust of the arena or the applause of the
crowd; the falseness of open compliment, the
insincerity of unspoken blame. His language
should be judicial, or he should be silent. Now,
whatever may have been the merits or charm of

Lord Coleridge's American utterances, no one will be disposed to call them judicial. His praise of many things American may be fairly held extravagant; his eulogy of Matthew Arnold is open to the same objection ; while, if the American press be correct, he even attempted socially to whitewash General Butler, Governor of Massachusetts, the most unscrupulous and indecent of demagogues, whose defeat during the late elections has delighted all honest men, whether Republicans or Democrats. His ungrudging praise of the judiciary of the United States altogether ignored the fact that a considerable proportion of that body, elected by the same processes as give municipal government to the cities, is notoriously inefficient and corrupt, and that the criminal classes, who are personally most interested in the verdicts of the courts, select the judges to preside in them. Even in lighter matters Lord Coleridge's desire to please went somewhat in excess of the requirements of the situation. His comparison of English and American beauty, which occasioned much comment in the States, cannot be considered just to his own countrywomen. The *Washington Post* says :—

"But his expressions regarding the American ladies have imperilled the Lord Chief Justice's chances of ever again

finding favour in the eyes of English beauty. An absence of
only two months from his native land has served, he says, to
win him from the standard of English loveliness, and he can
conscientiously champion only the American type of beauty.
Wherever he went the American lady was the same charming
personage, and the American girl the same self-possessed
bundle of independent anomalies. He could not sufficiently
praise the fresh complexions, the charming manners, and the
independence that marked the ladies he counted himself fortunate in meeting. And fairly turning against his own
countrywomen, he unhesitatingly admitted that in his eyes
the American women were the more attractive."

A correspondent of the *New York World*,
who claimed to have interviewed Lord Coleridge
on the steamer which took him to England,
writes :—

"He said he thought the American women far excelled
their English cousins in both beauty and intellect, and he
should not be backward to say so on his native soil."

Although justice be proverbially blind, and the
ethics of compliment are elastic, there is no occasion to believe that Lord Coleridge ever made the
remarks attributed to him in so crude a form ;
and American reporters are very apt to record the
questions they may ask as being the answers they
have received. But the comparison, whether made
by Lord Coleridge in these terms or not, is one
of some interest, and a few remarks on it will not
be out of place. There can be no doubt that

Americans honestly believe their women to be the most beautiful in the world ; nor to them would there appear any extravagance in the remark of the *New York Sun* on the audience which attended Irving's first performance, " in respect of the beauty it contained far surpassing any audience that Mr. Irving ever bowed to in his life." But the opinion of foreigners—I do not speak of Englishmen alone —is very different ; and I have never met one who had lived long or travelled much in America who did not hold that female beauty in the States is extremely rare, while the average of ordinary good looks is unusually low. More pretty faces are to be seen in a single day in London than in a month in the States. The average of beauty is far higher in Canada, and the American town in which most pretty women are noticeable is Detroit, on the Canadian border, and containing many Canadian residents. In the Western States beauty is con-spicuous by its absence, and in the Eastern towns, Baltimore, Philadelphia, New York, and Boston, it is to be chiefly found. In New York, in August, I hardly saw a face which could be called pretty. Society was out of town, but an estimate of national beauty is best formed by a study of the faces of the people ; and the races at Monmouth Park had collected whatever of beauty or fashion

E

had been left in the city. Even at Saratoga, the most attractive face seemed that of a young English lady passing through on her way to Australia. In November, New York presented a different appearance, and many pretty women were to be seen, although the number was comparatively small, and, at the Metropolitan Opera House, even American friends were unable to point out any lady whom they could call beautiful. A distinguished artist told me that when he first visited America he scarcely saw in the streets of New York a single face which he could select as a model, though he could find twenty such in the London street in which his studio was situated.

The American type of beauty is extremely delicate and refined, and London and Continental society will always contain some American ladies who may rank among the loveliest in the world. Such are known to us all, but are more common in Europe than America. A beautiful girl is, in the first place, more likely to travel than a plain one, for she is anxious for new worlds to conquer; the pride and affection of her parents are more likely to second her legitimate ambition, and, having reached Europe, she is obviously more likely to remain there. If American girls be anxious to marry Englishmen, as a study of

contemporary novels, plays, and society would
seem to show, it is a proof of their good sense ;
for America, which is the best place in the world
for making money, is the very worst for spending
it.   Life revolves round the office and the shop
and the counting-house, and a woman of spirit
doubtless prefers a society like that of London,
where even the men, to say nothing of the women,
from the time they rise at eleven till they go to bed
at three o'clock in the morning, think of nothing
but how they may amuse themselves. America
will grow day by day more like the Old World
in this respect, and when its citizens shall have
learned the science of amusement it will become
a far more agreeable place than it is at present.
The change in the habits of the men will have a
direct effect upon the beauty of the women.   The
English are an athletic race, and the amusements
in which they delight are in the open air.   As are
the men so are the women.   Riding and rowing,
walking and tennis, have developed in them a
beauty the chief charm of which is that it is
healthy.   The late hours of the ball-room do not
take the bloom from a cheek which is daily renewed by a gallop in the park before luncheon
or a game of lawn-tennis in the afternoon.   In
America life is sedentary.   The national game of

base-ball is mostly played by professionals ; the national pastime of trotting-matches cannot be counted as exercise in the English sense of the word. The men, with few exceptions, have no country life—few of them even know how to ride ; they neither hunt nor row, nor shoot, nor play cricket; and the women, being everywhere the shadow of the men, are accomplished in none of those outdoor exercises in which their English sisters find and renew their beauty. The charm which is born of delicacy may be a very lovely thing, like the finest porcelain, but it does not constitute the highest form of beauty, which is inseparable from good health.

The foregoing remarks, which were intended in all courtesy, excited, on their first publication, much angry criticism in America. Denunciation of political profligacy was not only expected, but could not equal in acrimony that which daily appeared in every American newspaper. But it was an unpardonable offence to challenge the superiority in beauty of the American women over the rest of the feminine world. One or two extracts may be taken almost at random from American journals. *The New Orleans Times Democrat* writes as follows :—

"His denial of the beauty of American women does not call for any special mention. That is a matter of taste, and an opinion is valuable in proportion to the qualifications of the judge. Sir Lepel may prefer the large and ample style of his countrywomen to the more delicate types of this country. It is his privilege to do so, and its exercise may possess for him the additional attraction of placing him in antagonism to nearly every foreigner of taste who has visited the country. No doubt the arrangement is gratifying to so thorough a Britisher as Sir Lepel Griffin appears to be. It is quite evident that he would be shocked and grieved to find himself forced into agreeing with the rest of the world. We can afford to dismiss this topic without making an effort to dislodge any of our critic's convictions. His proposition that American women are unhealthy and that the average Englishwoman is a model of grace and beauty is simply amusing and nothing more. He is welcome to his preference, and, as he declares his horror of dwelling anywhere save in England, we are rather disposed to congratulate him on his philosophy."

A Chicago newspaper writes :—

"The pertinence of what Sir Lepel has to offer upon this delicate subject depends entirely upon his standard of beauty, and these standards always vary in different localities. The Central Africans regard the Caucasian pink and white as something hideous. The ebony hue is to them the colour of beauty. The thick lips, the sprawling noses, and the kinky hair express to them the highest type of loveliness. In like manner the Mongol luxuriates in the saffron hue and almond eyes, the long finger-talons and pinched feet as the traits which go to make up the symbolic Venus. The Digger Indian regards the squalid, splay-footed, disgusting belle of his tribe as a thing of sweetness and light. What are Sir Lepel's standards ? Probably the English women. We hope it is not ungallant to say that if they are no one will be surprised to learn that he does not think American women are handsome. Measured by English standards they certainly are not. Fortunately we

have had opportunities of applying the tests. They sent us
their most lovely lady—widely advertised as the professional
beauty of England—sent her over here making no pretensions
that she was an actress, but claiming for her that she was
lovely beyond all description or comparison. Her charms
had distracted all England and had been praised by all
the connoisseurs and esthetes from the Prince of Wales to
Oscar Wilde.

" The ' Jersey Lily ' came, and it was soon found that she
could not compare in beauty with scores of American ladies
in every city where she was on exhibition. Her charms
smote one of our countrymen to a considerable extent and at
considerable expense, if reports be true, but the rest of the
population escaped unscathed. Having had the typical
English beauty on inspection, we can speak with some
confidence in the matter.'·

Criticism of this character would seem wanting
in precision if it be remembered that nowhere in
her own country is a beautiful American woman
more admired than in English society. The
history of successive London seasons proves
this ; and the passion of the English for novelty,
which has.been noticed by every foreign observer
from the time of Froissart, inclines them rather
to exaggerate than depreciate the attractions of a
fair stranger. All can remember American ladies
who have been accepted as beauties in London
drawing-rooms where far lovelier English women
have remained unnoticed. It is improbable that
any civilised or cultured person, whose eye, or
ear, or mind has been trained in accordance with

the acknowledged rules of art and taste, would be influenced in his estimate of beauty by national predilections. Does the Englishman prefer the daubs which cover so large a space on the walls of the Royal Academy to the glories of the Pitti or the Vatican ? Does the cultured American prefer the thin milk and water of Mr. W. D. Howells to the strong wine of Thackeray or George Eliot ; or ignore the winning grace of Ellen Terry for the pastoral friskings of Minnie Palmer ? I think not : and Englishmen are ready enough to allow that in some parts of Italy, in Greece, and on the northern shores of Asia Minor the average of female beauty is far higher than in his native land. National vanity, where inordinately developed, may take the form of asserting that black is white, as in France, where the average of good looks, among both men and women, is perhaps lower than elsewhere in Europe. If a pretty woman be seen in the streets of Paris she is almost certainly English or American : yet if a foreigner were to form an estimate of French beauty from the rapturous descriptions of contemporary French novels, or from the sketches of *La Vie Parisienne*, he must conclude that the Frenchwoman was the purest and loveliest type in the world, in face and figure. The fiction in this case disguises itself in no semblance of the truth.

I have freely admitted the American type of beauty to be extremely delicate and refined, and, although I maintain my position that there are more pretty women to be met in London in a day than in the States in a month, yet the comparison thus made is hardly fair to America, seeing that London naturally absorbs all that is best and brightest in English men or women ; and there are many parts of England where beauty, among the lower classes, is as rare as in America. Moreover, the ranks of London beauty are swelled each season by a large and distinguished American contingent.

Many of my critics have disputed the statement that American women are delicate and physically undeveloped ; but denial does not affect those notorious facts which the physicians of the States themselves endorse. But on this subject I would neither wish nor presume to speak, though, in justification of my former statement, I will venture to quote the words of a few American authorities whose unprejudiced opinion would seem convincing. To them I will only add the expression of a hope, which all friends of America will share, that a more healthy and robust physical training of children and a growing love of exercise and field sports, may restore the race to the vigour of its original stock, and avert the now threatened danger of physical decadence.

Dr. S. Weir Mitchell writes :—

" To-day the American woman is, to speak plainly, physically unfit for her duties as woman, and is, perhaps, of all civilized females the least qualified to undertake those weightier tasks which tax so heavily the nervous system of man. She is not fairly up to what nature asks from her as wife and mother. If the mothers of a people are sickly and weak, the sad inheritance falls upon their offspring, and this is why I must deal first, however briefly, with the health of our girls, because it is here, as the doctor well knows, that the trouble begins. Ask any physician of your acquaintance to sum up thoughtfully the young girls he knows, and to tell you how many in each score are fit to be healthy wives and mothers, or, in fact, to be wives and mothers at all. I have been asked this question myself very often, and I have heard it asked of others. The answer I am not going to give, because I should not be believed—a disagreeable position in which I shall not deliberately place myself. Perhaps I ought to add that the replies I have heard given by others were appalling."

Later he continues :—

" Now I ask you to note carefully the expression and figures of the young girls whom you may chance to meet in your walks, or whom you may observe at a concert or in a ball-room. You will see many very charming faces, the like of which the world cannot match—figures somewhat too spare of flesh, and, especially south of Rhode Island, a marvellous little-ness of hand and foot. But look further, and especially among New England young girls : you will be struck with a certain hardness of line in form and feature, which should not be seen between thirteen and eighteen at least.   And if you have an eye which rejoices in the tints of health, you will miss them on a multitude of the cheeks which we are now so daringly criticising.   I do not want to do more than is needed of this ungracious talk ; suffice it to say that multitudes of our young girls are merely pretty to look at, or not that ; that *their destiny is the shawl and the sofa, neuralgia, weak backs, and the varied forms of hysteria,* that domestic demon which has produced untold discomfort in many a household, and, I am almost ready to say, as much unhappiness as the husband's dram."

Dr. Allen, of Rhode Island, speaking of the strictly native New Englanders, says :—

" The women have deteriorated physically in a surprising degree.   A majority of them have a predominance of nerve tissue, *with weak muscles* and digestive organs."

The New York *Sun*, in commenting on this statement of Dr. Allen, says further of the New Englanders who have remained at home :—

" Their families are small.   They are not physically as vigorous as their fathers.   *The women are not symmetrically developed, and their nervous organisation is apt to be morbid.*"

The statements of the Rev. S. W. Dike :—

" The diminishing size of the New England family of so-called native stock is well known.   The reported number of children of school age in Vermont and New Hampshire is scarcely three-fourths as large as it was thirty years ago."

The following is the opinion of Mr. William Blaikie :—

"The results of this utter neglect of any sound system of physical education stand out in almost every city home in America. Scarcely one girl in three ventures to wear a jersey, mainly because she knows too well that this tell-tale jacket only becomes a good figure. Yet the difference in girth between the developed arm which graces a jersey and the undeveloped one which does not, in a girl of the same height and age, is seldom more than two inches, and often even than one, while the well-set chest outgirths the indifferent one by seldom over three inches. Among girls, running is a lost art. Yet it is doubtful if an exercise was ever devised which does more to beget grace and ease of movement. There are probably not ten girls in any class of fifty in one of our public schools who could run a mile, even if they got a dollar a foot for it. Or twenty boys out of any fifty either."

Later, in his clever article on "Our Children's Bodies," the same writer compares the physically robust Canadians with his delicate countrywomen :—

"In what contrast with this make-believe walking and the wofully defective physical culture and condition of many of our city girls is the story told in the following despatch from the Montreal Carnival last winter :

"'Next came skating races, which were only second, in drawing spectators, to the trotting. As is universally known, Montrealers are like ducks, who take to the water when born. They assume skating frolics when escaping from the cradle. It is literally true that they are skating almost before they are able to walk. The fascination in the exercise, which seems to be hereditary, increases as they grow up, and when they have arrived at manhood or womanhood—*for the girls are even*

*more expert than the men—they can rival the world for grace
and agility as runners.*   Proof of this last assertion was seen
by thousands on the river this afternoon.   The contests were
in some cases more tightly fought out than by the trotting
equines.'

"What a ring and tingle and glow of ruddy health there
is about all this !   We wonder if those girls know what a
headache is, or a side-ache?   Or if 'the shawl, the sofa, and
neuralgia' are likely soon to be their destiny ? . . . .
How would, not the weakest and most inert, nor yet the fleetest
and most enduring girl, but she who fairly represents the
average girl in one of our school classes, have fared in that
inspiring struggle that bright winter afternoon on the gleaming
broad St. Lawrence?   Would she have been in it at all, much
less anywhere near the front rank, at the end of half a mile,
or even of a quarter?   Ask her brother, and he will tell you
plainly—whatever different and more flattering version some
other girl's brother may make of it."

When we read of these performances of the
Canadian girls, and, further, of the lady who has
been accepted in the States as the representative of
English beauty, astonishing the Americans by a
thirty-mile walk without fatigue, we can understand the belief held by Englishmen that delicacy
directly detracts from beauty, which is inseparable
from good health.

In reply to the statement that the English standard of beauty is incorrect, it may be suggested
that it is in strict accord with the most ancient
examples and the generally accepted canons of
art, and that a study of classical models will show

that Greece and Rome, in their worthiest days, acknowledged no beauty which did not include full physical development. The lithe and willowy figure, the praises of which are sounded by American writers, and the grace of which has an undoubted charm, too often represents mere physical degeneracy.

Nothing is more pleasant in America, or places the civilisation of the country in a brighter or more honourable light, than the universal respect publicly paid to women by men of all degrees. That there is in this something of exaggeration, and that some women abuse their exceptional privileges, demanding discourteously what men are ready voluntarily to offer, does not materially affect the question. An American gentleman who resigns his seat to a lady in a steamboat or tram-car, or who wearies himself in looking after her luggage and wrestling on her account with railway porters, does not ask even the thanks which politeness should be eager to proffer. His action has been disinterested, instinctive, and to satisfy his own sense of propriety. The difference, in this respect, between the French and American Republics is curious indeed. A Frenchman will ruthlessly turn a lady into the mud of the street rather than step off the pavement himself; or will bribe the railway guard to

induce delicate women to leave their pre-engaged
carriage in order that he may not sit with his back
to the engine.   He will hardly assist a woman in
distress unless she be attractive.   The French,
below the thinnest veneer, are the most impolite of
civilised races,   Americans, on the other hand,
though without superficial polish, are warm-hearted
and chivalrous in the highest degree. The position
in which they have placed their women is the best
guarantee that the nation will outgrow the blemishes
which now disfigure it, and will, in the future, attain
a higher civilisation than has been enjoyed by any
people who have regarded their intellectual and
political life as the undivided dominion of man.

But the emancipation of women is not without
its dangers and inconveniences. Between woman
and man there can be no true equality, for there are
no common terms to express what is essentially
different ; and, if the woman allow her social and
domestic position to be undermined, her victories
in other fields will avail her little. And of this
there are some ominous signs in America. Within
the last thirty years, divorces in the States have
doubled proportionally to population and the
number of marriages. Being granted for trifling
reasons, such as incompatibility of temper, and
the law governing them being different in the

several States ; while the confusion is increased by
a vast immigration of strange nationalities,
wandering hither and thither in search of a
favourable settlement, it can be no cause for
surprise if the fixity of marriage be shaken and the
conception of the family as the social unit becomes
weakened in favour of the individual. But this
result, so far as social evolution is concerned, is
strictly retrogressive. The feeling against Mor-
monism is, in the States, exceedingly strong ; and
polygamy is, beyond dispute, a condition unfavourable and indeed fatal to a high civilisation,
although the community of Salt Lake City must
be allowed to be prosperous and well ordered. But
a too facile divorce law differs from polygamy in
little but name, and some American writer has said
that the man who has three or four wives divorced,
one after another, only drives his team tandem,
while the Mormon elder has it four in hand. The
proportion of divorces to marriages is in some
States startling enough. In San Francisco city
there was a divorce to every five marriages in
1881 : in Maine, there were 507 divorces in 1880,
or nearly one to nine marriages. The frequency of
the suits results in the utmost carelessness of the
courts ; in one State the average duration of such
cases is fifteen minutes. At Chicago, according to

Mr. Henry Ward Beecher, the boys on the train call
" Chicago, thirty minutes for divorce," and though
I cannot say that I have myself heard them, the
incident is not more surprising than was the touting
for clients of rival parsons of the Fleet, in the
London of the last century.   Collusion becomes a
matter of course ; the tie which can be so easily
snapped is inconsiderately formed ; while the
frequent difference in the law renders it difficult to
know whether the marriage or divorce of one State
is valid in another, and induces many foreign
immigrants to abandon their families and marry
elsewhere.   The evil of the present state of things
is so great and acknowledged that ere long
Congress will be compelled to intervene and pass a
uniform law for the whole United States. England
may take a lesson from America in this particular,
that, so far as divorce is concerned, the sexes are
equal before the law.   Here, where the subjection
of women has so long formed a discreditable chapter
in the statute book, from which a higher liberalism
and a more chivalrous generosity have not yet
completely banished it, the relief which men can
demand is refused to the weaker sex which needs
it the most.   Equal justice will not, it may be
hoped, be much longer denied ; while divorce will
be granted for cruelty, habitual intemperance,

or on conviction of any heinous or disgraceful crime.

The idea which underlies the institution of marriage has materially differed in England and America, whose first chivalrous settlers abandoned all they held most dear in order to avoid the heavy burthen which sacerdotalism, ever allied with tyranny, had placed upon them. They rejected marriage as a sacrament, and regarded it as a civil contract, the moral obligation and permanency of which would have till now remained undisputed had not the flood of immigration and the rapid development of the country formed a solution so strong as to partially dissolve social institutions, as it has those political methods which were sufficient for the original community. In England, on the contrary, the idea of marriage as a sacrament has survived its exclusion, as such, from the Anglican ritual; and its acceptance as a civic contract alone, secure, like other solemn engagements of a formal character, under an impartially administered law, is only gradually taking the place of the former sentiment. The conservatism of the country is ever too strong for the speedy triumph of any liberal principle; and sacerdotalism, as distinct from religion, is still an imposing force. It must not be imagined that

F

the priestly caste, of any denomination, is more liberal or charitable in America than elsewhere. The trail of the serpent is over them all. Cotton Mather and his Puritan fathers preached as savage a gospel as the Spanish Inquisition, and his descendants are worthy of him. Last October a Congregational minister named Newman was preaching in New York on "Christianity triumphant in the elevation of Woman." The representative of Independence and Dissent furnished and produced all those old weapons of sophistry which English ecclesiasticism is being forced to abandon. He pronounced for the sacramental character of marriage, and ridiculed the civil ceremony. Here he was assisted by the fact that, besides the denominational ministers, the New York aldermen were empowered to perform it. "Imagine," he said, "a New York alderman performing such a ceremony. A New York alderman with a shillelah on his shoulder, brogues on his feet, and potatoes in his pocket. A walking grog shop, reeking of gin. Surely such a marriage performed by such a one is scarcely worth seventy-five cents." The roars of laughter which greeted this description sounded oddly in a religious building. The apostle of hatred then proceeded to denounce the Mormons, who, he said, defied the laws of the United States, and urged that the heresy which had grown up in the West should be forcibly trampled out. It would have been more to the purpose had he denounced the practical polygamy and polyandry which result from the present condition of the marriage law.

It cannot be denied that the position of women in the United States is far more favourable and just than in England, where their most elementary rights have been only lately conceded in the Married Woman's Property Bill. Their equitable claim to such work as they may choose and can efficiently perform is not disputed, and the unmanly riots in Kidderminster to prevent the employment of women in the curtain and carpet manufactories would hardly be possible in America. For them an elaborate system of higher education, technical and industrial, has been framed ; and, three years ago, there were no less than 227 high-class institutions, besides colleges and universities, in which women could study as completely as men, chemistry, geology, botany, physics, mathematics and all such applied sciences as might be useful to them in private or professional life. Most of these institutions are

F 2

the growth of the last twelve years ; and, as
England has made a good start in this most
honourable contest it may fairly be hoped that
she will not permit America to leave her behind.

Whether the emancipation of women has not
proceeded too far in the case of unmarried girls
is a question which those who are acquainted with
American society can best decide. I confess a
preference for the English system, which, midway
between the complete and jealous seclusion of
France and the independence of America, allows
the young girl as much liberty as experience has
shown can be safely intrusted to her. American
novelists have described their young country-
woman as formed of different clay to the rest
of the world, and so strong, self-reliant, and
superior to the infirmities and weakness of
humanity as to be able to defy the dangers
which may threaten her from without or from
her own heart. But the American girl is still
one of Eve's family, and as susceptible as any
of her European sisters. The process known in
England as "keeping company," and confined to
the humbler ranks of life, is an institution of
American society ; and an unmarried girl can
receive her admirers without reference to her

parents ; and drive or go to the opera or theatre
with the special object of her attention. Marriage
is the original object of this as of all customs,
civilised or savage, which bring the-youth of both
sexes together ; but pleasure rather than marriage
is the modern development of the idea. A young
débutante in New York or Boston, in her first
season, when her attractions are the brightest and
her chances of marriage are naturally the best,
is adopted by one of the professional male flirts,
who may be a gentleman of good position and
whose attentions flatter the vanity of the in-
experienced girl. He is her constant attendant at
balls and picnics, in public and private. He may
not have the remotest intention of marrying, yet
drives out of the field the aspirants who would
propose. These intimate relations, which would
not be tolerated for a day in England unless the
parties were engaged, may continue the whole
season, or for two ; or may be repeated with
another or half-a-dozen newer admirers. If this
system be liked by American men, there is no
reason that any one else should object to it. But
that it must tend to rub the bloom off the peach,
and lessen the delicacy and freshness of a girl's
sentiments is obvious to all who know anything

of the world or the human heart. Men, unambitious
in their social aspirations, would prefer a wife from
a New England farm-house to a New York beauty
who had been ostentatiously protected through a
whole season by a Fifth Avenue exquisite.

CHAPTER V.

EQUALITY.

THE doctrine of equality, essentially illogical though it may be, has, in America, been carried into practical effect so far as the conditions of social and political life will allow ; and in no other country can its results be more clearly seen or more accurately tested. There can be no study more interesting than the strange and wide divergence in the application of the doctrine in the two great Republics of to-day, France and America. In the former we are accustomed to the emblazonment on every public building of the republican profession of faith, *Liberté, Égalité, Fraternité;* but what is the interpretation of the legend ? Liberty, as reflected in contemporary French literature, is the apotheosis of animalism, of which Zola's latest novel is the most loathsome witness ; equality signifies the internecine warfare of class against class ; while fraternity is hardly more than a

deeper contempt and a keener hatred of everything not French. The Republic has given to
France little beyond a perpetual change of street
nomenclature, and a more greedy class of officials ;
it has not deeply influenced the life of the people,
and may be thrown aside to-morrow like a coat
which has outlived the fashion. A theatrical air,
suggestive of the footlights, attends it, and thus
it has failed to attract the sympathy of America,
whose sturdy and ingrained Republicanism de-
spises the democratic tinsel and limelight. There
was a time when Paris was the veritable paradise,
not of women alone, but of the whole American
race; when the pinchbeck glories of a brand
new court, whose welcome of parvenus was
naturally sympathetic, fluttered the gentle breasts
of the Yankee matrons and maidens, whose ideas
of society had been formed in the quiet of New
England villages, or amid the bustle of Saratoga
caravansaries. But with the fall of the Empire
the love of Americans for Paris grew cold, and it
is amusing to hear them describe the ruin which
republican institutions have wrought in their
latest paradise, after the same fashion as Satan is
held to have made the first uninhabitable. They no
longer see Paris clothed in the old imperial
glamour, but as it really is—a commonplace, stucco

wilderness, as dull and sordid as their own New York ; where the theatres are crowded dens sacred to asphyxia, and the opera house a stupendous imposture, where gilding usurps the place of art : a city where the only sentiment ennobling the population is expressed in the daily effort to make as much out of the foreigner as possible, with the least expenditure of money or politeness.

Equality is understood in America in a very different sense. Not there, as in France, the expression of a passing caprice, it is the monomania of an entire nation. An ideal impossible of attainment, contradicted in daily practice by the exclusive society of New England and the South, as by the millionaires whose monopolies are its very negation, it yet influences the life of the people in every particular, much as the belief that he could fly governed every movement of a lunatic I once saw in an asylum. The struggle after equality has determined most of the social institutions of the States : domestic service houses, hotels, cuisine, travelling and education. It has dominated their politics and has perhaps determined their religion. It has withdrawn much of the sweetness and light from their social life, and has left literature and art as monotonous a wilderness as their own prairies.

The first relation affected by the worship of
equality, and one which underlies every social
condition in the United States, is that of master
and servant. This, in its patriarchal or modern
English sense, can hardly be said to exist in
America. If, by law and in popular belief, one
man be the equal of another, it necessarily follows
that the position of the servant, or help, to the
citizen who pays him for certain specified service
is essentially different from that which he holds in
countries where tradition and prescription have
attached to menial service other conditions than
the bare performance of particular duties. The
first and the most important of these is the outward observance of unvarying respect to the
master. This habit of deference, which would be
termed servile in America, has in it no necessary
element of servility. The relations between a
well-bred Englishman and his servants are cordial
and mutually respectful ; with them he is not
familiar, but neither is he arrogant or unreasonable.
The prescription of a thousand years has decided
that they move on different though parallel lines ;
they do not approach, but neither do they collide.
Here, the divisions between the different classes
are almost as complete as those which separate the
castes of India—those immemorial barriers against

change which only those would remove who do not understand that they insure the stability of our Eastern Empire. When in England a successful tradesman gives up business and buys an estate in the country he breaks altogether from his former moorings. He will not be received with open arms by the county families, and if they do not return his calls, his isolation is complete. But the neglect of the exclusive caste does not affect the behaviour of the menial class towards him; and his footmen are as obsequious and dignified as those of his aristocratic neighbours. However much Boston or Virginia may proclaim their high descent—pretensions which seem somewhat out of place in a Republic—or however contemptuously the exclusive clubs of New York may regard the enriched parvenu, there are no recognised castes in America. Mr. Macgillicuddy, the ex-grocer, with his house in Fifth Avenue and his wife and daughters brilliant with diamonds, has changed position but little from the time when he bullied his shop boys in Broadway. Indeed his personal interest in the shop continues; for were he to be idle he would find no one to keep him company, and would probably die of *ennui*. And as there is no caste of masters, so is there none of service. The advantage of the feudal tradition which prevails in

England is, that domestic service being held in no dishonour, and implying no loss of self-respect, it has grown into a science to be perfectly acquired by patience and study alone. The exclusiveness and fastidiousness of a cultivated and wealthy class have produced the perfection of domestic service, performed with the least possible friction, by persons as accomplished in their menial but still honourable duties as the masters in their several occupations. In America there is nothing of this, and the absence of quiet and respectful service is to an Englishman an ever-recurring source of annoyance. No one can deny that the American ideal is a noble one, and worthy a great and free people. Every political dogma which encourages the true man to rise above the evil surroundings of his birth or his misfortunes, and look his fellow, without fear or favour, in the face, is worthy of respect, and the doctrine of equality has distinctly raised the character of the mass of the American people. The servility which is too often the disgrace of Europe is unknown; and, among the many fine qualities of the Americans, none are more honourably conspicuous than their courage, frankness and independence.

So strongly do I feel this that I would not wish my observations on some practical applications of

the doctrine of equality to be considered as hostile
criticism, but rather as passionless comment on
curious phases of national life. For to English
prejudice—and prejudice it may be—equality is
a bitter pill to swallow. I remember a family who
sold their possessions in England for a settlement
in the Western States. The soil was favourable,
the climate congenial, and they might have grown
to love their new home but for the one circumstance that they were compelled to take their
meals with the farm labourers. It was no feudal
survival, with the master above and the servants
below the salt ; all were socially equal, and their
helps would at once have left them had they been
relegated to the kitchen ; so, after a prolonged
struggle with these, to them, impossible surroundings, they sold their farm and returned to
England, poorer if not wiser than they left it. In
the Northern States, the Irish and negroes almost
monopolise domestic service, but the first are un-
trained and the latter are only efficient within
narrow limits. So difficult and indeed impossible
is it to procure good servants that the whole style
of living has been affected by it. The houses are
strangely small ; and in a city as wealthy as New
York there are very few which in London would be
considered of the first rank. The spacious family

mansions, which in London are to be counted by thousands in the western quarters, hardly exist in New York. Fifth Avenue—which, with a few off-shoots, forms the fashionable quarter—contains but few houses above the average of those in a London square. Country houses, in the English sense of the word, with great establishments of servants of every grade, are unknown. The New York million-aire, whose wealth makes so imposing a show in London or Paris, lives at home in what we should consider a very modest fashion. He inhabits a house of a dozen rooms, and is served by four or five helps. His house is small because he cannot procure good servants; or his servants are few as his house is not large enough for a great es-tablishment. There should here be some room for compensation. An English gentleman with an income of £100,000 a year will keep up a large London house and two or three places in the country, the expenditure on which swallows up the greater portion of his income. Hence it is that the English aristocracy are so little dis-tinguished for acts of public beneficence; and landlords who amass millions from the ground rents of London do nothing to beautify the metropolis in which they should take a special pride, and the dignity of which they should

associate with their own. The great benefactions
to the public, colleges, parks, obelisks, and squares,
are the honourable gifts of merchants and manu-
facturers, of stock-jobbers and vendors of quack
medicines. The American millionaire, who by no
personal extravagance can spend his income, might
be expected to devote a considerable portion of it
to the public good. But this is the last thing of
which he thinks ; and it is only fair to remember
that riches make to themselves wings and fly
away with strange rapidity in America. The
money easily won is easily lost, as the history
of Monte Carlo may remind us ; and the pile of
many a Yankee millionaire has been made in
a manner quite as speculative and no more
honourable than the chances of the gaming-
table.

The American town house which is too small
to accommodate an establishment of servants
is obviously too small for a governess, so the
daughters of the family, deprived of that careful
home training which is held to be essential in
England, are exposed to the roughness and the
independence of a day-school, often in company
with boys of the same age. The effect of this on
the young American, of either sex, is not attractive,
though if American parents approve the system,

with its freedom and development of individuality, no one else has any right to complain. But I believe that it is only approved, because, under existing conditions, it is impossible to adopt any other; and the independence of their children, which to outsiders seems to savour of disrespect, is unnoticed by Americans, who have grown so accustomed to it that it has ceased to wound American children are wonderfully bright and clever, but their good manners are too often conspicuous by their absence.

Equality, which makes it impossible to procure service at home, induces a great part of the community to reside in hotels, which form a far more important feature in American than in English life. The American hotel is to a well ordered establishment of the same name in Europe what a six franc *table-d'hôte* meal at a Paris caravansary is to an artistically conceived dinner at the Café Anglais. Some are better, some worse; the Fifth Avenue Hotel or the Potter Palmer House at Chicago compare un-favourably with Barnum's menagerie, while a very few are distinctly good, such as the Windsor in New York, which is probably the best in America, with some of the old-world politeness, and one of the only cooks hitherto discovered on the new continent. The typical American hotel is as splendid as colour and gilding can render it; for the law of republican simplicity has determined that all public institutions, such as railway cars, steamboats and hotels, shall be decorated in the fashion which commends itself to the ornate taste of the shoddy millionaire, rather than to the more sober requirements of his poorer fellow-travellers. The ground floor, entrance hall, drinking bar and reading-rooms constitute the 'agora' or public meeting-place of the entire adult male population. Here at mid-day and at night they assemble to discuss politics, the stock exchange and the last murder; to quarrel, and smoke, and spit, and liquor up; and the bewildered traveller passes with difficulty through their noisy ranks to the counter where the hotel clerk, like Rhadamanthus, sits supreme above the babel, issuing decrees which are without appeal. This young man has formed the frequent target for American humour. He is said to have been originally created to fill the throne of an emperor or a dukedom, but there being few of these vacant has condescended to accept temporarily a position behind the hotel register. But, like the Peri, he does not forget his lost paradise, and his austerity, indifference to the public, and ignorance of every matter which can

G

be referred to him is probably unsurpassed. He is fortunately more insolent to his own countrymen than to Englishmen who, not being accustomed to salaried incivility, are more disposed to resent it. Having secured his room, in which every colour and every article of furniture will be an outrage on good taste—for the protective tariff compels hotel managers to patronize native manufactures—the traveller finds himself an unregarded unit in the crowd. Service in the proper sense does not exist ; and he will find it difficult to get his boots blacked unless he descend into the nether regions and have them polished on his feet. The dining-rooms, as the ground floor, are open to the public ; as indeed are the drawing-rooms, called in Irish fashion (which indeed is the origin of nine-tenths of so called colloquial Americanisms) the parlours ; but these last are deserted, so far as the male sex are concerned. After dining, they retire to smoke and drink, and the emancipated half of the world is left to enjoy its freedom alone.

The difference between the English and the American hotel is in the comparative privacy of the former. There are now, in London, hotels, built or building, as large as any in New York, several with upwards of a thousand rooms, but they are practically closed to the public. Each visitor is as secure from outside intrusion as if in his own house. The idea of making the hotel the common lounge for the loafers of the street corner and the drinking bars has fortunately not yet commended itself to English managers.

The American traveller pays a fixed sum for board and lodging, a system which has many advantages. It is on the whole cheap, and the traveller knows precisely what will be the amount of his bill. But it demoralizes the national cuisine, which is a department into which democratic ideas should not be permitted to enter. The American people being as accustomed to feed at public tables as the Spartans, and the *table d'hôte* being accommodated to the simplest palate and the shortest purse. the result has been that (putting clubs and private houses apart) cookery is an unknown art in America. There is abundance indeed, but it is the Homeric abundance of quartered oxen and sheep roasting whole on the spit. Roast and boiled in endless variety ; fish, flesh and fowl ; dishes so numerous as to satisfy the appetite of a Cyclops, but hardly anything fit to eat. The first thing brought by the waiter at every meal is a glass of iced water, in itself sufficient to spoil both dinner and digestion. The victim is then persuaded to declare the ten or

G 2

twenty dishes, from the endless menu, of which
he will partake ; and he is fortunate if he can
prevent the waiter from bringing them all at once.
Ordinarily the diner is seen surrounded by the
numerous dishes of his choice, eating against time
to prevent the *entrées* getting cold while he is
swallowing his soup. It is not the custom to
drink wine at dinner, and this alone is fatal to
the artistic conception of dining. The drinking
is done at the bar, after meals, standing ; in the
most unwholesome manner, and of the most unwholesome materials—the hundred mixed liquors
which are known to fame as American drinks, and
which by themselves account for any amount of
dyspepsia and ill health. The coloured waiters
are far more polite and attentive than their white
comrades ; but in America, as in Europe, money
will do much ; though the traveller, if wise, will
distribute his largess on arrival instead of on
departure, and can thus ensure, if liberally in-
clined, as good attendance as he can desire. The
Americans do not ordinarily fee the servants ; but
without this precaution, the foreigner may starve
in the midst of plenty. There is one restaurant
in New York of world-wide reputation—Del-
monico's—at which the cuisine is only good by
comparison with the general monotony of bad

cooking, though it is asserted to be superior to any establishment in London or Paris.

In travelling, the doctrine of equality has been tempered by the enterprise of Mr. Pullman, whose saloon and sleeping cars form, to all intents and purposes, a separate and higher class, although this idea is abhorrent to true Republicanism. However this may be, the rich and the poor, except on those less important lines which know not Mr. Pullman, are as much separated in travelling as in England. To compensate for this deviation from Republican principle, the emancipated negro attendant will endeavour to illustrate and assert the law of equality by taking his seat in the car, placing his dirty boots on the opposite cushions, and generally acting as new-born freedom suggests; and, in New Mexico, I have sat at dinner next to the engine-driver, who was a most worthy and amusing citizen, and to whose presence only hypercriticism would have objected, had he condescended, before joining the ladies and gentlemen, to remove the grease and soot from his face and hands. The person who in America impressed me as possessing power of the most absolute kind, before whose authority that of the President himself seemed to pale, was the railway guard, or conductor. Even the hotel clerk is a less

imposing personage in the Republic. Travelling
many thousand miles through the States, I watched
the conductor under many conditions and on many
lines of railway ; but I do not remember to have
seen one who was ordinarily civil or who had the
faintest knowledge of any subject connected with
the line on which he was employed. Where or
when the train stopped ; where refreshments were
to be procured ; at what junction the traveller
should change carriages ; on all such subjects his
mind was a blank. The railway company which
employed him was a monopoly which systematically disregarded and despised the public by which
it prospered, and he too acknowledged no obligation of politeness or information. He did not
consider himself paid to be civil or to answer the
wild questions of unreasoning travellers who ought
to purchase enigmatical guide books and discover
for themselves the mysteries of the road.

Nothing is more striking than the patience with
which the free American citizen bears the insolence
of office ; the rudeness of ticket-collectors, the
unnecessary violence of the police, and the general
contempt of every petty *employé* of the government or of private companies, who, one and all,
seem to consider the public they serve as a beast
of burden to be beaten or driven at their pleasure.

We are accustomed to this official aggressiveness and petty insolence in France or Italy, but it seems strangely out of place in an Anglo-Saxon Republic. For this temper is altogether foreign to the people. There is no more kindly and considerate person in the world than the unofficial American. Hospitable, generous and warm-hearted, he will take infinite trouble to assist a stranger, and if you ask him to direct you in the public street, will probably walk far out of his way to point out your destination. But politics have so demoralised office that with its possession his whole temper seems changed. The old wine of authority is too strong for Republican bottles, and next to being an official yourself, there is hardly a greater misfortune than to have to conduct dealings with one.

One of the most curious social results of equality is the supposed right which it gives to one portion of the community to interfere with the private and domestic concerns of another. Even the President of the United States is not above such interference. Mr. R. B. Hayes was a total abstainer, and nothing stronger than lemonade was to be procured at the White House during his occupancy. When President Arthur, a temperate and courteous gentleman, succeeded to office, a committee of ladies is said to have waited upon him and informed him that he must drink only water; but he courageously informed them that he should regulate his dinner-table without their assistance. Not long since, the Free-Will Baptists of Minnesota passed a resolution warmly approving the noble and economical spirit of Mr. Hayes in serving water to his guests, and viewing "with growing alarm the use of intoxicants by President Arthur." This concern for the manners and morals of the highest officials, however impertinent, has not been altogether unjustified, for every citizen is a possible occupant of the Presidential chair, and may carry there the habits he has acquired during his earlier days of rail-splitting or cattle-farming. I remember a former President with whom sobriety was an exceptional, and indeed a phenomenal, phase of existence ; and a United States minister at a European Court who was too uncertain of the direction in which his legs would take him to receive the Royalties who had honoured his evening party.

When Presidents can claim no immunity from the shrill lectures of prohibitionist missionaries, it is clear that the rank and file of simple citizens cannot hope to drink in peace. Against this persecution the Germans have stoutly fought, and are prepared for any sacrifice rather than lose their national beer. Where they are most numerous the

prohibitionists have had least success ; but there
are wide districts in which no intoxicating beverage
is to be procured without a resort to humiliating
subterfuges. The people no doubt drink a great
deal, and most crimes in America, as in England,
have their origin in intoxication. But there are
few drunken people to be seen ; and whether the
liquor trade be a blessing or a curse, it is not for a
Republic which professes to uphold individual
liberty to insist upon people abstaining against
their will. We have, however, no occasion to cross
the ocean to see fervent Liberals preaching a com-
pulsory temperance in opposition to the true spirit
of Liberalism.

CHAPTER VI.

SWEETNESS AND LIGHT.

IT was with much interest and some anxiety that I went to Chickering Hall to hear Matthew Arnold's first lecture in New York, for he had freely condemned the Americans in former days as a race of Philistines, and they have long memories. We English are accustomed to Mr. Arnold when, like Balaam, he starts on a mission of cursing. Whether we drink champagne, or sand the sugar, or beat our wives, we know that there is no escape from condemnation. Unless we can take refuge with the few elect in his private ark, we belong to an upper class materialised, a middle class vulgarised, or a lower class brutalised. But the Americans were not used to this drastic treatment, and had shown some temper when told that, even if they had fewer barbarians and less mob, they were an unredeemed and irredeemable vulgar middle

class. Chickering Hall, however, displayed no
signs of hostility. On the contrary, when Mr.
Parke Godwin had ended a laboured and perfervid
introduction, the great English critic was received
by a crowded house with every sign of sympathy
and respect. There was not a vacant chair, and
the audience was evidently largely composed of
the most educated and cultured classes, and included many ladies. But the lecture, as such,
was a complete failure. Matthew Arnold says he
dislikes public speaking, and certainly his voice is
—or was—unequal to the demands of a well-filled
hall. Reading his lecture with the manuscript
close to his eyes, placing a strong accent on the
penultimate or ante-penultimate syllable, and
dropping the last altogether, allowing the voice to
so sink at the close of a sentence that the last
words were inaudible, without gesture or expression, Mr. Matthew Arnold combines in himself all
the possible faults of a public lecturer. Sitting
ten rows in front of the reader, I found it impossible to hear the whole of any sentence or to follow
the argument of the address. Occasionally, a
quotation more or less familiar could be picked
from the general monotone—as Dr. Johnson's
declaration that "Patriotism is the last refuge of
a scoundrel," or Plato's description of Athenian

society : " There is but a very small remnant of
honest followers of wisdom, and they who are of
these few and have tasted how sweet a possession
is wisdom, and who can fully see the madness of
the multitude, what are they to do ? "

But these were mere oases of sound in a desert
of inaudibility ; and of the fifteen hundred persons
present, perhaps a hundred understood the lecture,
to some four hundred an occasional sentence was
vouchsafed, while a thousand heard nothing.   An
American audience is wonderfully patient and
generous ; and although at first from several parts
of the hall came unavailing cries of " Louder,"
" Can't hear you," yet, when it was thoroughly
realised that remonstrance and entreaty were in
vain, the audience resigned themselves to the
enjoyment of their Barmecide feast in a manner
both amusing and pathetic. The lecture, if audible,
would hardly have satisfied an American audience.
Its purport seemed to be that majorities were
always vicious and wrong; and that the only
advantage to America in her great and increasing
population was that, in so vast a multitude of fools
and knaves, there must be a considerable "remnant"
who, if fortune were favourable, which the lecturer
did not anticipate, might redeem and transform the
corrupt mass.   Mr. Matthew Arnold is very likely

right, but with these sentiments America has no sympathy. It holds that he wastes his rare powers in futile criticism of the Philistines, who are the practical men of the world and who do its real work. The night after his lecture, the well-known journalist, Mr. Dana, in the same hall, repudiated his doctrine, and declared that the facts of America and Europe contradicted his theory; that in England and France there was little or no political progress, that in democratic institutions and the principle of equality were the salvation of the human race; while material triumphs by man over nature contained the condition of progress, a work independent of poets and essayists like Mr. Arnold. There can be no doubt that Mr. Dana truly interprets the feeling of his countrymen, who are satisfied with themselves and do not care to be improved or instructed by any teacher, however illustrious. Mr. Matthew Arnold, piloted by Mr. D'Oyley Carte, and inaudibly lecturing to New York society, too painfully recalls Samson grinding corn for the Philistines in Gaza.

If the future of America were of little importance to humanity, the inquiry as to whether its inherited or acquired sweetness and light satisfied the severe demands of Mr. Matthew Arnold would have no more interest than the disputes of mediæval casuistry. But the destiny of this great country and this brave and energetic race is of supreme importance to the world, and especially to England. Before children now born shall have grown grey there will be but three Great Powers in the civilised world : the Greater Britain, Russia, and the United States. France, Germany, and Austria may still be prosperous and maintain vast standing armies as to-day ; but to the Anglo-Saxon and the Slav races will have fallen the dominion of the world. We have thus a direct interest in ascertaining the direction in which American civilisation tends, and the force and sweep of the currents which reach our shores from the western side of the Atlantic. Of what temper is this strange creation, whose origin was indeed due to England, but over whose growth she has had no control ? Is it a monster, like that wrought by Frankenstein, eager to confuse and destroy; or is it but a new avatar of the Goddess of Liberty, who has softly lit, dove-like, with white shining wings, on the western shore ? The more urgent of these questions will best be answered when we later consider the tendency of the political institutions of the United States. Here I would only touch on those lighter subjects, culture, literature, and art, which are suggested by Mr.

Matthew Arnold's visit to America, and which have an influence only second to political institutions on the mental and moral growth of a people. Culture is essentially aristocratic in the highest and unconventional sense of the term, and flourishes best among a class whose inherited wealth and leisure permit them to find their interest in intellectual pursuits rather than in money-making, which is the most absorbing as it is the most demoralising of occupations. Art is, in a great measure, dependent on patronage; and, if the art is to be worthy, the patronage must not be of the uneducated multitude, but of the instructed and cultivated, who are everywhere few in number, but who will be found most rarely in democracies. The Bonanza king of San Francisco, who is reported to have successfully sued a railway company for having delivered to him a cast of the Venus of the Louvre without the arms, which he insisted should have accompanied the goddess, may, under instructed direction, stock museums with foreign works of art, but cannot aid the development of native talent. The political bias of republics to equality; the popular dislike of inherited rank and wealth ; the redistribution of acquired property, all react unfavourably on culture, and discourage the growth of the leisured and refined class in whose existence is the best hope for the creation and the appreciation of works of art. It cannot be denied that there have been times and places in which there seemed to exist a phenomenal love of art among the people generally, as in Athens and Florence, which were republics in name though aristocratic in spirit; but although the popular taste was refined in these cities, yet the community affected was small, and had been educated to a high sense of beauty by the enlightened munificence of wealthy or noble families. The natural capacity of European races for artistic representation of beauty differs, not only in degree, but in kind ; and it is not likely that Anglo-Saxons will ever, in music, painting, or sculpture, reach the standard of Greece or Italy, though they have no superiors in literary achievement. It might have been supposed that the free air of a republic would be favourable to every class of intellectual effort ; and that its citizens would easily surpass those countries where knowledge is held in chains, or where authority, fashion, and prescription restrict on every side the movements of genius. But this assumption would not be supported by history, which shows that in England and France, the most active intellectual periods, richest in works of the highest imagination and power, were those when despotism was the rule of government, and reverence to authority was most conspicuous in the people. The truth seems to be, although the question is deserving of more attention than has yet been paid to it, that the atmosphere of a republic is unfavourable to art. The lamp of artistic truth burns with a feeble flame ; and mediocrity is allowed to take the highest place. The general level is so unbroken that it is difficult for Genius to find any elevation from which to take its flight. The absence of height to train the mental eye, injures the sense of proportion, and permits an exaggerated estimate of artistic excellence. If a careful and impartial review of the intellectual productions of the United States since their foundation, or during the last hundred years, be made, it will be found that, in no department of art, has any work, drama, novel, poem, painting, or musical composition been produced which could justly be placed in the first class. In science, America has been more distinguished, as might have been expected from a practical people devoted to industrial pursuits. But the absolute dearth of all work of the highest artistic value is most striking. In literature, there are many names justly held in honour and some authors whose

H

works have won a wide reputation ; essayists and historians as Irving, Emerson, Bancroft, Prescott, and Motley : poets like Bryant, Longfellow, Whittier, and Lowell : and novelists like Cooper, Holmes, Hawthorne, and Howells. Yet, although some of these writers have attained that mastery over style which Matthew Arnold seems to consider the chief sign of literary power, placing men like Addison, La Bruyère, Cicero, and Voltaire, in the front rank of letters, no American has, so far, shown himself possessed of constructive or imaginative power in any high degree. The stormy history of the young Republic, and the natural beauties of a new Continent have inspired no national poem ; nor indeed any poetry which can be ranked as of the highest order. Twenty years ago, in England, the poetry best known and most delighted in, after Tennyson, by the majority of readers was that of Longfellow, and its popularity was well deserved, for its simple charm, and pure, lofty spirit appeal directly to the heart. But when compared with his English contemporaries Tennyson and Browning, it is at once seen within what narrow limits the genius of Longfellow is confined. In dramatic work, which is the highest and most imaginative expression of literary genius, America has done nothing whatever ;

though it must not be forgotten that England, during the present century, has been almost as barren of high dramatic ability. Even in the dramatic representations of the stage, American artists appear ordinarily devoid of that imaginative power which enables the actor to so seize and embody the very life and individuality of a character as to touch spectators with that swift and sudden sympathy which makes of the dramatic art the very mirror of nature. Booth, and to a less degree, Jefferson, may be held to possess something of this power, but it is altogether absent from the work of most American actors, as might be seen this season in London, where Mary Anderson and Lawrence Barrett have drawn large houses : one, as a pretty and picturesque woman, the other as an accomplished and well-trained artist, without possessing the power of stirring the faintest emotion in the spectators or conveying any impression of reality in their several parts. That this defect is less inherent in the actor than due to the unsympathetic and uncongenial atmosphere in which he has been trained, seems likely when it is remembered that the majority of American actors are English or Irish by origin, and indeed the American stage is as rich in brogue as if it were recruited direct from Cork. The low ebb of the dramatic art in America is the more striking from

the wide and deep love for the theatre among the
people. In no country are there more numerous,
better arranged or more handsome theatres, or
more enthusiastic and quick-witted audiences.
Every point is at once appreciated by the house ;
and dramatic criticism is often both learned and
discriminating.

The chief hope for American literature and art
is, that as they outgrow English influences, they
may become more robust and national. No one
would wish to deprive our kinsmen across the
ocean of their common inheritance in the glories of
English literature, which forms the most powerful
of the ties which bind us in amity together. But
the overpowering splendour and richness of that
literature have had an enfeebling and crushing
effect upon American writers. Year by year,
English influence grows visibly less, and this is
a healthy sign. Even the extravagant estimate
placed in America on the work of some contemporary native authors, which, judged by our
standards, appears worthy of but small admiration,
shows the growth of an independent national spirit
without which no literature can be excellent or
durable. In other departments of art, where
English influence is necessarily weak, such as
painting and sculpture, Americans are advancing
to an honourable place ; though they do not draw

their inspiration from native air, but from Paris and
Rome. In music, their time has not yet come;
though, as the best of so-called English music, now
taking a high place in the artistic history of the
century, is Irish in origin, and as there are more
Irishmen in America than in Ireland itself, it may
be hoped that republican surroundings may not
forbid its successful cultivation there.

There can be no more potent means of increasing and deepening popular culture than by the
introduction of art into the common ways of
domestic life; employing taste and beauty to
dignify the most ordinary articles of furniture,
ornament, and dress. In this direction, free trade
has done much for England, and of late years the
standard of good taste in domestic life has greatly
risen. But, in America, the protective tariff has
prevented the general use of foreign manufactures
with the consequence that most of the work is crude
and inartistic. Whether a love of beauty has, as yet,
taken much possession of the English people may
be doubted; but improvement is everywhere visible,
and comfort and good taste are becoming, every
year, more common in the homes of the English
artisan. I will conclude this chapter with an
extract from the letter of the American correspondent of the *Pittsburg Dispatch*, who had been
sent to England to examine into the question of

wages and labour, and which from such a source is especially interesting. I would particularly commend it to the attention of English working men, who are disposed to think their own class is more favourably situated in the States than in England. It deals with a subject by no means foreign to "sweetness and light," for wholesome and well-ordered homes are the soil from which true culture must spring.

" A walk from Wolverhampton, with its 100,000 inhabitants, to Birmingham, with its 400,000, is through a succession of villages, which form an almost continuous town, through a forest of chimneys which send forth pillars of cloud which obscure the sun by day, and pillars of fire which outshine the moon at night. The vast bulk of the smoke is outside of Birmingham, so that it is less beclouded than one would anticipate from its reputation. It is not by any means so enshrouded as the ' Birmingham of America ; ' but its smoke and soot are not hemmed in by high hills, but are constantly dispersed by the breezes from the Channel and the Welsh mountains. Yet in this field are manufactured not only incomputable quantities of raw iron and large machinery, but thousands of kinds of small articles in immense bulk, guns, swords, all kinds of brass and ormolu articles, jewellery, presses, pins, buttons, bicycles, needles, fish-hooks, money, not only for the Home Government, but for a dozen other governments, and innumerable other things which one always knew were made somewhere but never knew the place.

" And now, let me say briefly, and once for all, that a careful inspection of the localities where working people most do congregate in this wonderful world of manufactures, has proved to me, as it will prove to any one taking similar pains, that here, where one expects to find ' pauper labour,' by comparison with America there is a condition of comfort in habitation, clothing, and food, which cannot be excelled in any American manufacturing locality. This may be treason, but if it is, my protectionist friends are at liberty to make the most of it. I do not assert that the condition of these workmen is what it ought to be. I only assert that if it be worse than that of American workmen, then the difference is concealed with wonderful success. I am not advancing by any means the opinion that it is time to apply the theory of free-trade to America, but merely reiterating what I have often said and always believed, that the assertion of republican politicians that protection was in the interest of the working-man was buncombe, for if it was of any benefit at all the working-man got none of it, but the capitalist all. If I was not altogether certain of my premises then, I am now. I will agree to exhibit better houses for working people, with just as ample food and comfortable clothing, and as many bank depositors in this Birmingham district, according to ratio of population, as can be found in any manufacturing district of America. It would make the most prejudiced and most loyal Pittsburger ashamed of his own city, to note here the actual superiority in comfort and cleanliness of the streets and houses where live the common working classes. Courts, alleys, and domiciles are clean, and lack the foul odors which are smelled everywhere on the back streets and alleys of Pittsburg. I searched in vain for a plague spot. I asked for the localities where there were the most poor, and went there ; I propounded all sorts of impudent questions to the inhabitants ; I penetrated to the obscurest courts and alleys, making inquiries for imaginary persons my excuse, and my conclusion was that, so long as we must have a poor class—a class which must struggle hard for bare necessities—it would be well to have them live as they do here, if possible. Everything, too, speaks of good government. Hell-holes, such as exist in some parts of Pittsburg, seem to be unknown here. The gin-mills and tap-rooms are compelled to close promptly at the hour fixed by law. To judge from the police statistics, crime is here reduced to a minimum."

CHAPTER VII.

THE HARVEST OF DEMOCRACY.

SOME two years ago a political satire was published in New York under the title of *Solid for Mulhooly*,[1] which did not receive from English politicians the attention which it undoubtedly deserved. It was not to be seen on the club tables in Pall Mall, nor was it in demand at Mudie's, and is now, I understand, out of print. Nevertheless, its interest is so great, and the conclusions which seem naturally to follow its story pierce the soul and marrow of modern English politics with so true and acute a rapier-point, that representative Radicals like Mr. Chamberlain, or disguised Radicals, as is Lord Randolph Churchill, might well republish the work for gratuitous distribution in the still unenlightened and unregenerate constituencies. *Solid for Mulhooly* purported to be a

---

[1] By Rufus E. Shapley, of Philadelphia.

new and novel satire on the Boss system in
American politics, in which the mysterious
methods of the leaders, the Ring and the Boss,
were laid bare ; and although, for the American
public, which the chief living exponent of the
science of political corruption asserts to have
greater patience and longer ears than any other
animal in the New World, there could be little
that was novel in the revelations, there is much
which is, fortunately, both new and useful for
Englishmen.

It cannot be expected that the arid wilderness of
American politics should ever become a fair and
pleasant garden in which English students may
wander with delight and contentment. The subject is strange and distasteful, and from most points
of view unprofitable, and Americans themselves
turn from it with disgust. If but few educated
Englishmen could explain the differences in dogma
between the Republican and Democratic parties,
an average American could do little more, seeing
that to the eyes of impartial observers the only
conflict between political parties is as to which
should obtain the larger proportion of the spoils of
victory — the fat offices given to unscrupulous
wirepullers ; judgeships, the reward of the prostitution of justice ; and contracts by which the people

pay three dollars for every one which is expended
on its behalf.

There is, however, one light in which American
politics have for Englishmen an engrossing interest,
namely, the effect which democratic principles,
carried to their extreme logical conclusions, have
had upon a race identical in many particulars with
the English from which it has sprung. Has this
effect been such as to encourage us to apply these
principles at home ? Has the result been a nobler
view of the obligations of citizenship ; a more
generous and unselfish use of wealth ; a higher and
purer municipal administration ; a more patriotic,
farsighted, and courageous foreign policy ? And
even should a favourable answer be returned to
these inquiries, there remains for Englishmen the
practical question whether, if undiluted democracy
be suited to the conditions of America, with its
vast homogeneous territory and a population still
scanty proportional to its area, secure from all
foreign attack and self-contained and self-sufficient
in its resources, we could reasonably expect that it
should be equally successful in England. For this
country is the centre and *omphalos* of a world-wide
empire, confronted in every land and on every sea
with enemies or rivals ; with an overgrown population crowded into cities and dependent on others

for their very bread, and already enjoying a system
of government which is not only the envy of less
fortunate peoples, but which has had the force to
make us, and may still possess the inherent virtue
to maintain us, first among the nations of the
earth ?

A novel called *Democracy,* giving a clever and
amusing sketch of Washington society and the
political intrigues which have their origin and
development in the capital of the United States,
excited considerable interest in England a short
time ago.   It was written with much spirit, and its
frankness was so condemnatory of American institutions that it was first supposed to be written
by an Englishman.   But there are no more severe
critics of their political system than the Americans
themselves, and the authorship of *Democracy* is no
secret at Washington, where I have met more than
one of the persons whose presentment is supposed
to be given in the novel.   Another book lately
published—*A Winter in Washington*—though of
doubtful taste, and below criticism as a work of
literary art, is fully as outspoken regarding the
low tone of morality which prevails in political
circles.   But, *Solid for Mulhooly,* the work which
I have taken as the text for this article, is of a
different quality.   Its style disdains those half-

lights and shadows and reticences which belong
to romance, the conventional glamour which
artistically obscures the naked truth. It carries
the American political system into the dissecting-
room, and pitilessly exposes the hidden seat of its
disease. While *Democracy* shows the ultimate
result of official corruption in the lobbies and
drawing-rooms of Washington, *Solid for Mulhooly*
discloses its genesis in the drinking-saloon and the
gutter. *Democracy* differs from it as a rainbow
differs from the mathematical formulæ which
express the laws that determine its shape and
colour. A short sketch of the plot, showing
how a penniless adventurer became Member of
Congress, rich without toil, like the lilies, in-
fluential without character, and famous through
his very infamy, will not be unprofitable.

Michael Mulhooly was born in those conditions
which experience has shown to be eminently
favourable to prominence in American statesmanship—a mud cabin among the bogs of County
Tyrone, which he shared with his parents, his
ten brothers and sisters, and the pig. Fortune
sent him early to America, where his struggles
and subsequent successes form the subject of the
story. Epitomised as was his history by the
journal of the Reform party, it read thus:—

"A bogtrotter by birth ; a waif washed up on our shores ; a scullion boy in a gin-mill frequented by thieves and shoulder-hitters ; afterwards a bar-tender in and subsequently the proprietor of this low groggery ; a repeater [1] before he was of age ; a rounder, bruiser, and shoulder-hitter ; then made an American citizen by fraud after a residence of but two years ; a leader of a gang of repeaters before the ink on his fraudulent naturalisation papers was dry ; then a corrupt and perjured election officer ; then for years a corrupt and perjured member of the Municipal Legislature, always to be hired or bought by the highest bidder, and always an uneducated, vulgar, flashily-dressed, obscene creature of the Ring which made him what he is, and of which he is a worthy representative ; such, in brief, is the man who has been forced upon this party by the most shameless frauds as its candidate for the American Congress. This is filthy language, but it is the only way in which to describe the filthy subject to which it refers, as every man who reads it must admit that it is only the simple truth.

"Is it possible that the American people are compelled to scour the gutter, the gin-mill, and the brothel for a candidate for Congress ? Is it possible that the Ring which has already plundered the city for so many years, and which has so long abused our patience with its arbitrary nominations of the most unworthy people for the most honourable and responsible offices, will be permitted to crown its infamies by sending to Congress this creature who represents nothing decent and nothing fit to be named to decent ears ?"

---

[1] Repeating is an amusing game much played at American elections. The repeater, who, if possible, should be a professional bully and prizefighter, represents himself to be and votes for some member of the party opposed to that which employs him. When the true voter appears at the poll he is assailed as a fraudulent person who desires to register twice, and is kicked and beaten by the repeater and his friends. This game causes much innocent amusement.

Though all this, with much more that the indignant journal wrote, was not only true but notorious, it had no effect upon the foregone conclusion of the contest. The Boss, who held in his hand the fifty thousand Irish Catholic votes of New York, called upon one of the judges whom he had "made" to convict of libel the journal which had dared to tell the truth and condemn his favoured nominee. Justice was dishonoured and the truth was condemned. Meanwhile the campaign was fought between honesty and corruption. The candidate of the Reform party was a young man of good family, the highest character, possessed of wealth, genius, and eloquence, and he had at his back all the voters of respectability and position. But he did not condescend to those arts which could alone insure success. He did not visit bar-rooms, or drink with and treat the party-workers, or bribe or cajole; and he declared war to the knife against the Boss and the Boss system, and the Ring, and the whole gang of confederated thieves who had for so long laughed at and plundered the people. The result was what might have been foreseen. The leaders, the Ring, and the Boss, and their thousands of dependents, were "solid for Mulhooly," who was elected Member of Congress by the grace of the municipal gods; manhood suffrage was vindicated, and the corrupt, obscure adventurer represented "a Government of the people, by the people, and for the people."

It will be asserted that this satire is exaggerated, and a caricature of the truth. But this is not the opinion of those educated and high-principled Americans with whom I have talked in the large cities, such as Washington, New York, Philadelphia, Chicago, Minneapolis, or Denver. They are generally willing to discuss the political situation with all frankness if they be only approached with discretion. Should the traveller commence with abuse of American institutions he will naturally meet with a rebuff; but should he sympathetically praise an administration which professes to be of and for the people, his listener will quickly open the floodgates of his invective against it. From my Colorado note-book I extract the *ipsissima verba* of one of the most prosperous and distinguished citizens of that State. "Politics," said he, "are nothing but a trade by which to live and grow fat, and an evil and a stinking trade. No one who respects himself can join it, and should a respectable man be chosen for office he refuses to accept the nomination. Everything connected with it is corrupt ; and success being impossible to an honest man, the dirty work is left to the scallawags and scoundrels who live by it, and who degrade the name of politics throughout America."

The City of New York has, for many years, been one of the most striking and convenient illustrations of what is known in America as Boss rule, and the many millions that it has cost the people, in waste, peculation, and undisguised and unblushing robbery, form the price which they have had to pay for the pretence of freedom. Matters are now less openly scandalous than of old, but the same system is in full force. Boss Kelly, who sways the destinies of New York, has been able, from his near connection with an Irish cardinal, to defend his position with spiritual as well as temporal weapons, and the whole Irish Catholic population vote solid as he bids them. The result of a generation of this *régime* has been disastrous. The commercial capital of the United States may now be fairly reckoned, for size and population, the second city in the world, if Brooklyn, New Jersey, and the suburbs be included within its boundaries. Its property is assessed at fifteen hundred million dollars, its foreign commerce is not far from a

billion dollars, while its domestic trade reaches
many hundred millions.   But there is hardly a
European city of any importance which is not
infinitely its superior in municipal administration,
convenience, beauty, and architectural pretensions·
With the exception of the Post Office and the
unfinished Catholic cathedral, which is neither in
size nor design a cathedral at all, there is scarcely
a building which repays a visit.   The City Hall,
which cost ten or twelve millions of dollars, is
certainly worth inspection as an instance of what
swindling on a gigantic scale is able to accomplish ;
as is the Brooklyn Bridge, which cost seventeen
millions, or three times the original estimate, and
which was further unnecessary, as a subway would
have been more convenient and have cost much
less.   Local taxation is crushingly heavy, and so
inequitably assessed that the millionaires pay
least and the poor most.   The paving of the
streets is so rough as to recall Belgrade or
Petersburg ; the gas is as bad as the pavement ;
and it is only in Broadway and portions of Fifth
Avenue that an unsystematic use of the electric
light creates a brilliancy which but heightens the
contrast with the gloom elsewhere.   The Central
Park, so called from being a magnificent expanse
of wilderness in the centre of nothing, is ill-kept

I

and ragged, and at night is unsafe for either sex. The fares of hack-carriages are four to five times as high as in London. The police is inefficient, arbitrary, and corrupt. At its head are four Commissioners, who are politicians in the American sense and nothing more. They are virtually appointed by the aldermen, who have authority to confirm or reject the mayor's nomination of heads of departments. The aldermen are, in many cases, persons to whom the description of Michael Mulhooly might apply—politicians of the drinking-saloons, the tools and slaves of the Boss who made them and whose orders they unhesitatingly obey. When a respectable mayor has chanced to be appointed, he has declared it useless to nominate good men to office, and has lowered his appointments to the level of the confirming aldermen. The Comptroller, who is the financial head of the city, expending between thirty and forty millions of dollars annually, the Commissioners of Excise, Taxes, Charities, Fire, Health, and Public Works, are all controlled, approved and virtually appointed by the aldermen, who are directed by the Boss. Even the eleven police judges, who should be the independent ex-pounders and enforcers of the criminal law, are appointed by the same agency, so that if their origin be traced to its first cause they are the nominees of the criminal classes they have to try and punish. The result is that it is impossible to procure the adequate punishment of any official, however criminal, since he was appointed as a political partisan. One or two instances, almost at random, may be cited in illustration of this. While I was in New York a policeman, named McNamara, killed a drunken but perfectly quiet and inoffensive citizen, named John Smith, by blows on his head and neck with a loaded club. There was no provocation, and even New York was profoundly moved by the outrage, although the police are there accustomed to use their clubs on even orderly crowds in a manner which would not be tolerated for a day in England. But while a verdict of murder or aggravated manslaughter would alone have met the merits of the case, McNamara was found guilty of assault in the third degree, and sentenced to a nominal punishment. In the case of the numerous catastrophes on railways and steamers in and near New York, due to gross negligence and causing the wanton slaughter of numerous citizens, no official has for years past been punished. An inspector's certificate is the only guarantee of security of the numerous passenger steamboats which ply on the waters of the city. But in August last, when the *Riverdale* steamer blew up and sank, the boiler was found so corroded that a knife-blade was easily thrust through a piece of iron which was originally an inch and a quarter thick ; while the inspector who had certified that the boiler was in good order stated on inquiry, that he did not know that the boiler was corroded because he had never examined the inside. Inspectors of this calibre are appointed to certify to the soundness of the boilers of ocean steamers, and the chief engineer of one of these told me that the inspector who had looked at the outside of the engines and had signed the required certificate, when asked whether he was not going to examine the interior of the boilers, confessed that such an examination would give him no information, as he was altogether ignorant of the construction of engines or boilers.

Nor are public interests and private rights in property more respected than personal safety is secured. In London we see Mr. Bowles fighting against a railway which is to pass underneath the parks without once appearing at the surface, and even those who consider his zeal excessive will yet admit that this jealousy of any invasion of popular rights is wholesome and admirable. Yet, in New

York, elevated railways, on iron pillars level with the first-floor windows, have been run through many of the principal streets, without a dollar of compensation having been paid to any one. It may be that the ultimate result has been to raise the rents of the shops in these thoroughfares, but this does not alter the fact that the original construction was an outrage on the rights of private property and a hideous disfigurement of the public streets.

The carcase over which the New York vultures are now gathered together is the new aqueduct, which is estimated to cost from twenty to thirty millions of dollars, but which, if the precedents of the County Court House and the Brooklyn Bridge be followed, will probably cost sixty millions. Here is a prize worthy of Tammany and a contest —a mine rich in jobbery and corruption for years to come ; and there is no doubt that, before the work is completed, many patriotic Irish statesmen of the Mulhooly type, who are now loafing around the saloons on the chance of a free drink, will be clad in purple and fine linen and cheerfully climbing the venal steps which lead to the Capitol.

The mal-administration of New York has, at the present time, a very near and personal interest for Londoners.   It is proposed by the Government to place the administration of the vast metropolis, with its limitless wealth and multiplied interests, in the hands of one governing body, which there is no reason to believe will attain a very high standard of wisdom, virtue, and administrative ability. The Guildhall Parliament will be no more than a glorified vestry, with its jobs and personalities and indifference to the public interest; and it is unlikely that candidates of distinction will present themselves or be elected should they be nominated. It is true that, in England, politics are still a profession for honest men, and on the London School Board many persons of eminence have shown themselves willing to perform arduous and ungrateful work for the public. But the experience of this Board is not altogether hopeful, and able and accomplished candidates have too often been rejected for pretentious busybodies. It will be the duty not only of the Government but of Parliament generally, to consider carefully the arguments from analogy for and against the London Government Bill, and to take care that the disgrace which has fallen both on New York and Paris by intrusting enormous responsibilities to corrupt, feeble, and interested municipal bodies may not attach to London which, with its many defects in organisation, is still incomparably the best administered of the great cities of the world.

The municipal administration of New York and many of the principal cities is injurious not alone for its inefficiency, robbery, and waste. The chief evil, and one which, like a cancer, is ever poisoning and corroding the yet wholesome body politic, is found in its contagious example. Theft and jobbery are exalted as virtues which lead to wealth and political honour, while honesty and wisdom are left to preach at the corners of the streets regarded by none. The name of the people, and manhood suffrage, and the popular vote, are used as veils to screen the shifts and frauds of wire-pullers; and the elected of the people is often no more than the corrupt nominee of a dishonest clique who laugh at the people, who, now, as ever, are willing to be deceived. Corruption accumulates on every side ; its slime makes every path slippery which politicians tread, till the State Legislature and Congress itself become an Augean stable which would require a new Hercules to cleanse.

Americans who love and are proud of their country, and who loathe the political system which degrades it in the eyes of the world, will not consider the picture that I have drawn over-coloured. But it is impossible to acquit even the most honourable among them of the blame which attaches to this state of things. Manhood suffrage, untempered by any educational test and rendered uncontrollable by the surging mass of emigration, which was a condition unestimated by the drafters of the Constitution, is the chief cause of the present difficulty, and respectable Americans do not see how they can escape from it. Their usual reply, when driven into a corner, is that although the administration is shamefully corrupt, they will be able to reform it whenever they have time to do so. At present they are engaged in making money as quickly as they can. They cannot be troubled with politics ; but when at leisure they will reform the administration and make it clean and honest. Moreover, the country is young, and people, like the English, who have passed through the political experiences of the Georges, should not be squeamish in criticising America, which is undergoing a not more discreditable process of purification. The double fallacy which underlies this defence is obvious to every historical student. In all communities, and certainly in America, the honest and respectable largely outnumber the disreputable and disorderly. Yet the greatest catastrophes in republics have been due to the cowardice and apathy of the

former when opposed by the organisation and
audacity of the latter.   The excesses of 1793,
both in Paris and the provinces, were the work of
a very small minority, who might have been easily
overpowered had the nobles and *bourgeoisie* shown
the commonest energy and courage.   The horrors
of the Commune were due to a handful of men
whom the shopkeepers of the Boulevards could
have driven into the Seine with their yard-
measures.   Safety is never to be secured by
hesitation and delay, and the longer an abuse remains unremoved the more difficult is its extirpation.
The conditions of political life in England during
the last century and those in America to-day are
essentially different   Here the power was in the
hands of an educated class, who, as the standard of
morality became more high, were compelled to
change their methods or lose power altogether.   But,
in America, manhood suffrage has placed power in
the hands of the lowest and least educated class,
a large proportion of whom have little sympathy
with the country of their adoption and are too
ignorant to understand its requirements.   Education may possibly affect these favourably in the
future ; but it is also to be considered that the
present system directly tends, by making dis-
honesty more profitable than political virtue, to

continually augment, in an ever-increasing ratio, the number of those whose interest it is to perpetuate the reign of corruption. Nor can America plead youth as an excuse for her moral decrepitude. A vicious and depraved youth does not promise a healthy manhood or an honourable old age. The advantages of her youth were a people unfettered by the chains of poverty and prejudice which weigh on the races of Europe, and a field free for the noblest experiments in government. She inherited the experience and culture of the ages; she could profit by their splendid examples and avoid the rocks on which they had made shipwreck. She should have advanced and not fallen back; and this was the proud hope of her earliest statesmen. The young and vigorous republic of the West was to revive the classic virtues of Brutus and Cincinnatus, and blaze forth, a pillar of fire, to guide through the darkness the effete monarchies of the Old World. But it would be difficult to name any country, except Russia, where the Emperor Nicholas declared that he and his son were the only people in the country who did not steal, and where his successor found that the chief peculator of the recent war was his own brother, to which the political history of America would not be a warning rather than an example.

While, in England, there is an intelligent and
increasing party who advocate the adoption of
universal suffrage, thoughtful men in America are
convinced that this very manhood suffrage, unac-
companied by an educational test, is the chief cause
of their misfortunes.   Mr. Trevelyan, at Galashiels,
speaking for the Government, recently declared
that their policy in the extension of the franchise
had nothing to say as to whether a man were
Whig or Tory.   "We say, if he is a householder,
fit to vote, he should have a vote.   We think that
every *intelligent and independent* head of a household should have an equal voice in directly choosing
the representatives and indirectly choosing the
Government of the country."   There is probably
no consistent Liberal who would not accept this
principle, which applies to Ireland with as much
force as to England.   But it is obvious that the
condition of fitness is its all-important qualification.
Mr. Trevelyan's distinguished uncle, in one of his
splendid sophistries, asserted that to deny men
freedom until they knew how to make a proper
use of it was worthy of the fool in the old story
who would not go into the water until he had
learned to swim.   But men who are unintelligent
and uneducated ; who have not shown themselves
possessed of temperance, honesty, and self-restraint,

are virtually infants who have not yet the use of
their limbs, and whose experiments in the water
can only end in their destruction.   Open wide the
doors of the franchise to education and intelligence,
but, with the example of America before us, close
them in the face of ignorance and crime.

It is popularly supposed that in no country are
the advantages of education more widely diffused
than in the States, and if this were the case, the
danger which now threatens the Republic from the
character of those into whose hands political
power has been placed would not exist.   But so
far as published statistics inform us the reverse is
the case.   A Bill is now before Congress to provide
Federal aid to education, the schedules of which
seem to show that the ignorance of the masses is
exceptionally dense.

Illiteracy holds the balance of power in fourteen
Northern and in all the Southern States.   In the
thirty-eight States of the Union there are no less
than 1,871,217 illiterate voters : only one voter in
five can write his name in the Southern States.
The illiterate voters in South Carolina are more
than one-half the entire number ; in Alabama,
Florida, Mississippi, Georgia, North Carolina and
Virginia one in two; while Missouri, with one in
nine, has the best record.   In the Presidential

election of 1876, New York, New Hampshire, New
Jersey, Connecticut, Indiana, California, Nevada,
Ohio, Oregon, Wisconsin, Illinois, Rhode Island,
Michigan and Pennsylvania were ranged on the side
of illiteracy.   In the last Presidential contest the
voters in thirty States, commanding 298 electoral
votes, were unable to read.   In 1876, 60 out of the
76 senators, or four-fifths of the whole, and 259 out
of 292 representatives in Congress, were in the
grasp of illiteracy.   In 1880, 58 out of 76 senators
and 292 out of 325 representatives were from
States where the illiterate voters held the balance
of power.   The most superficial knowledge of the
distribution of the white and coloured population
will show that these results are not primarily due
to the almost universal ignorance of the negroes.
It is so in States like South Carolina, Mississippi
and Lousiana where they outnumber the whites ;
and in Virginia, North Carolina, Georgia, Florida
and Alabama in which the numbers of the two
races are almost equal ; but in Connecticut, New
York, New Jersey, New Hampshire, Michigan,
Ohio and others, the negroes form a very small
fractional part of the population.   At the same
time, the incapacity of the negro for improvement
makes the question of the greater fecundity of the
black race one of extreme interest.   Their increase

proportionally to the whites is a matter of dispute, and Mr. J. H. Tucker, Member of Congress, has instituted careful inquiries, extending over the period from 1790 to 1880, from which it appears that the natural rate of increase of the whites is slightly greater than that of the blacks, and while the whites were 80·7 per cent. of the population in 1790, they were 81·5 per cent. in 1860. Including immigrants, the white population gained and the coloured lost 6 per cent. in the whole period from 1790 to 1880; while, in the last 20 years, the whites have gained 1 per cent; Texas being the only state in which the black population shows an increase. The outcome of Mr. Tucker's complete survey is that the white race composes 80 per cent. of the total population and is steadily gaining, but at so slow a rate as to afford no reason for expecting any material change in the ratio in the present or coming generations. Professor Gilliam, who has also made the question a subject of study, arrives at very different conclusions. He considers that the white population may be expected to double itself in 35 years, and the black in 20 years. In 100 years, this would make the black population of the Southern States 192,000,000, while the white would be only 96,000,000, and the white population of the entire country 336,000,000.

Professor Gilliam further considers that the greater fecundity of the negro race is due in a measure to the absence of those checks to population which exist in all other cases.

It is true, so far as statistics are reliable, that, if a period like the decade between 1870 and 1880 be taken, and the States and Territories in which there has been an increase be compared with those in which there has been a decrease, it will be found that, on an assumed basis of 100,000 whites, there has been a gain of 625 to the whites during the decade.   But it is probable that in the future the conditions which affect the white and black population will materially change.   The proportion between the two races for the last thirty years is shown in the following table :—

Year.	White.	Coloured.
1850	19,553,068	3,638,808
1860	26,922,537	4,441,830
1870	33,589,377	4,880,000
1880	43,404,876	6,577,151

These figures would, at first sight, seem to support Mr. Tucker's rather than Professor Gilliam's conclusions.   The white population has considerably more than doubled in the thirty years, while the black population has not done so.   The most remarkable feature of these figures is the slow rate of increase of the negroes between 1860 and 1870, and their rapid increase since the latter date, which has nearly overtaken that of the white population in spite of the advantage of European immigration, which, during the decade, amounted to no less than 3,129,384. When the probabilities of the future are considered, it appears reasonable to assume that the checks on increase, voluntary and external, will affect the white rather than the coloured portion of the community. The negroes will remain, as at present, uninfluenced by those moral and prudential considerations which, in educated communities, restrain the increase of population by discouraging early marriage or marriage altogether. These considerations will, with the white population, have an ever-increasing weight as the standard of living becomes higher and more luxurious, and the country less able to support the population without that struggle for existence which is seen in the older countries of Europe. While the prudential check will thus operate to diminish the ratio of normal increase, the same causes will affect the stream of immigration which will slacken and at length cease altogether. The race in population will then be between a reasonable and highly civilised people

restrained from marriage by numerous considerations of the most complex character, and an irrational and uncivilised negro community, whom
no prudential check on population affects, and who
can live and be happy on the simple elements
of sunshine and sweet potatoes.

K

CHAPTER VIII.

THE FOREIGN ELEMENT.

THE Irish question is as burning a one in American as in English politics, and I cannot help thinking it more hopeless in the States than here, from the difficulty of withdrawing concessions which have once been made. Mr. Edward O'Brien, in reply to a letter of mine in the *Times*, has insisted that the most progressive and prosperous cities in America—New York, Chicago, and San Francisco—are just those in which the population of Irish birth and descent is largest in proportion, and would have us infer that to this element their prosperity is chiefly due. As reasonably might we argue that the prosperity of London and Liverpool was due to the Irish, who are the poorest and most unmanageable part of their population. The splendid commercial situation of New York,

Chicago, and San Francisco, and the marvellous energy of the American population, are the cause of their prosperity. It is because they are rich that the Irish collect in them. They live almost exclusively in the towns, and although in Ireland they complain of not possessing land, yet in America they will not accept land for cultivation, though they may obtain it at a nominal price, or for nothing. The majority of the Irish of New York differ little from the same class in English cities ; they are mostly illiterate, and the secret of their power is not in their energy or numbers, but that the long and absolute rule of the priests has accustomed them to vote solid as they are bid. The voters of the city are two hundred and fifty thousand, and of these the Irish are probably little more than a fifth ; but the determination of their leaders, and their own ignorance and political ineptitude, enable the disreputable minority to triumph over the wealth, culture, and intelligence of the disunited majority. No more grotesque illustration of the failure of universal suffrage to attain the result which alone would justify it could possibly be found. The Irish Catholics of America are Democrats almost to a man, but this is an accident due to a national characteristic which is illustrated in the well-known story of the Irishman who being asked, on his first landing at New York, what were his politics, replied that he knew nothing of politics, but that he was against the Government. The Republicans having held office ever since the war, the Irish have naturally joined the ranks of the opposition. It would be a mistake to imagine that political purity prevails where there is no controlling Irish element. New York has been cited as a convenient illustration of the evils of the American system. But leave civilisation behind and go to the far West, to a new town, like Cheyenne, in Wyoming, and every form of electoral corruption will be found there rampant, and votes sold shamelessly and as openly as sheep in the public market. The Irish are far more unpopular in America than they are in England ; and little sympathy for their grievances is felt or expressed ; for the Americans are far too practical a race not to rate at their true value the utterances of interested demagogues such as O'Donovan Rossa and Parnell. The language used in Dynamite League meetings in New York, and the criminal actions which follow, are alike viewed with indignation and disgust by the whole American community ; but the weakness of Democratic Government is such that the respectable majority do not dare to crush or even silence these enemies of the human race, and allow them, without molestation, not only to preach and plot arson and murder, but to carry them into execution. No civilised Government should tolerate for a day the open preaching of murder, and America must not be surprised if her protection, not of political offenders, but of common assassins, results ere long in seriously straining her relations with this country.

It is a happy circumstance that the self-command and moderation of the English people are such that a long series of atrocious outrages has failed to arouse any wide-spread hostility to Ireland. Englishmen realise that Irish troubles are in great part due to the selfish and unworthy policy of past years, while it is impossible that the Irish should be unpopular when (putting *Messieurs les assassins* aside) there is no more delightful, lovable, and quick-witted race in the world. But we have not suffered from them as the Americans have suffered ; and were London, as is New York, in the hands of a gang of Irish adventurers, our patience might be tried too sorely. Mr. Parnell hopes in the next Parliament to command the political situation ; but as his avowed programme includes the rejection of allegiance to the Queen and dismemberment of the empire, he must not be surprised if both parties unite in temporarily, and so far as imperial questions are concerned, disfranchising constituencies who return members pledged to destroy and degrade the country. When the Irish leaders cease to demand what no party could grant them without immediate political suicide, they will find Englishmen disposed to render them full justice, and such a measure of local and municipal self-government as prevails in England, and is consistent both with imperial rights and with the duty of protection, we owe to the loyal minority in Ireland. When the time for considering this question shall arrive—and it will not be until the Irish leaders abandon the open profession of treason—the precedent of America, both in its war to prevent national disintegration and in the virtual independence of each unit of the Federal body, will doubtless receive full attention from the Liberal Government. In the ears of the orators of the Opposition, who habitually speak of the Irish as of some savage people with whom we were at open war, the words compromise and concession sound weak and criminal. But when History writes the annals of the nineteenth century and the voice of passion is still, the policy of the Liberal Government towards Ireland, its generosity in the presence of ingratitude, its justice and self-possession amidst the fierce storm of party abuse, will be held its best title to honour.

Since the above remarks were written London has been startled by the partial destruction of the Victoria Railway Station by dynamite, and by the synchronous attempt to destroy the stations of Charing Cross, Ludgate Hill, and Paddington. It has been curious to note the comparative indifference with which these crimes have been regarded by the people of London. There has been no panic and but little excitement ; while it has been generally felt that strong language directed against the dynamiters would be as illogical as abuse of wolves engaged in their natural occupation of ravaging the sheep-folds. The explanation is to be partly found in the enormous size of London, the districts of which know as little of each other as if they were situated in different countries. The unit in a body of five million persons regards with comparative equanimity an outrage directed against the entire community. The doctrine of chances protects him from being blown into the air. But while England watches with contempt the efforts of the dynamiters to pose as heroes in the eyes of the Irish helps of New York, whose wages they hope to divert to their own pockets, considerable irritation has been excited by the attitude of America. Indeed, the great Republic has never cut a more sorry figure; and its struggles to appear impartial, virtuous, and the sacred asylum of oppressed patriotism, are rather subjects for amusement than anger. The poor rags with which the New York Press has striven to cover its political nakedness are threadbare indeed. We are told that neither municipal nor international law meet the supposed exigencies of the case; that the law cannot act against the assassins without clear and irrefragable proof in each particular case; that no practical way out of the difficulty has been suggested; that political refugees must be protected, however objectionable their modes of argument; that the British Government declined to surrender Orsini, whose case was identical with that of the dynamiters, and that it would be illogical for England to expect America to take action where she had previously refused to move. It is possible that the American Government may be less timid than the Press, and may find sufficient courage to defy the Irish vote, and insist that those who live beneath its flag and claim its protection shall refrain from the open preaching and practice of murder—but a Presidential election is at hand, and those who

know America best expect least from its government. The *Alabama* precedent, in accordance
with which the English paid extravagant compensation for damage inflicted on American
commerce by ships of war which had been
allowed to arm in British ports, is, naturally,
declared in the States to be inapplicable. But
the nature of arbitration would not allow the
Americans to be themselves the judges of this
question ; and an impartial umpire, whether it
were France, or Brazil, or Germany, might hold
that the Government which allowed public sub-
scriptions for murder and outrage ; which saw
the assassins arrange their crimes, and glory, in
the face of the world, in their perpetration, was
fully as liable to be called upon for the amplest
compensation as was the British Government,
which, in a careless moment, and uncertain of the
power of its municipal law, allowed the *Alabama*
to leave its shores. There is no real doubt as
to the identity of the assassins. If a dozen men,
such as John Devoy, of the *Irish Nation ;* Patrick
Ford, editor of the *Irish World ;* P. J. Sheridan,
the friend of Mr. Parnell, and connected with
the same paper; O'Donovan Rossa and Patrick
Joyce of the *United Irishmen* were arrested and
sent to prison in default of sufficient guarantees

of future good behaviour, no great injustice would
be done.   But so long as the annoyance and
danger affect England alone, America does not
take the trouble to move.   The day will come
when American men and women and children
will suffer from the dynamiters' activity.   Then
Judge Lynch, whose methods Englishmen refuse to
follow, will have an interview with these New
York editors, ending with a short shrift and the
nearest telegraph pole.

The difficulties and dangers which necessarily
accompany manhood suffrage are, in America,
intensified by the enormous emigration and the
law of naturalisation under which aliens are
admitted as citizens after five years' residence.
The consequence of this provision, which, as in
the case of Michael Mulhooly, is frequently
evaded, is that a large number of persons are
annually admitted to all the rights of citizenship
before they have become American in sympathy
or sentiment, with the tendency to form separate
political groups looking only to the interests of
their own class or nationality.   Thus a number
of *imperia in imperio* grow up, German, Scandinavian, or Irish, bringing, as we have seen with
the last-named, confusion into the Federal Government, and fighting from beneath its shield against

their private enemies. The Germans, in America as elsewhere, are a sober, honest, and intelligent body, and have brought the land of their adoption its most valuable contingent. But they are rather in than of the American world. They do not intermarry with Americans ; they have their separate societies and amusements ; and as they now number some ten millions, there will at no distant date be a larger German population in America than in Europe, whose sympathies must more or less affect European politics. To a less degree these remarks apply to the Scandinavian emigrants, who, in States like Minnesota, are numerous. They have in no way changed their nationality with their climate, and the Swedish *chargé d'affaires* at Washington told me that they were continually referring to him in their difficulties instead of to the authorities of their State.

Difficulties such as these may be successfully solved ; but there is one legacy of the war, in the negro vote, which will only become more intolerable by the lapse of time, for the reason that the African race is extremely prolific, and, under existing conditions, may be expected to increase more rapidly than any other element of the heterogeneous mass of American citizens.

The position of the negro is anomalous and
embarrassing. Without referring to the multiplied
researches of the Anthropological Society on the
capacity of the African races, it may generally be
asserted that the negro is as fit for the franchise
as the monkey he closely resembles.   He has one
or two good qualities and many bad ones.   He
makes a very good waiter if in firm hands, but
is usually spoilt by American familiarity, which
in his small mind breeds contempt, so that the
head waiter at a restaurant give himself more
airs than an English duke. For any occupation
requiring higher intellectual powers than blacking
boots or waiting at table the vast majority of
negroes are unfit. A few of the best struggle
into the professions and there fail, though I
remember at Washington some cases of partial
success ; while one coloured female lawyer of much
vivacity roundly declared, during the recent civil
rights discussion, that the negroes were the
superior race in America.   Since the war they
have largely increased, and now number some
six millions of uneducated and unimprovable
persons, as useless for the purposes of civilisation
as if they were still wandering naked through the
African jungle.   Slavery is an accursed thing,
but it is rather as degrading the higher race of

slaveholders than as brutalising the slaves that it must be condemned. There is no more natural equality among races than individuals, and im-perial peoples have to use up some of the weaker and poorer in their political manufactories. The Nemesis of slavery was not exhausted in the civil war. Its evil fruits are still to be gathered by the American people, who have in their midst this ever-growing mass of savagery which they hate and despise, and to which they were com-pelled to give the rights of citizenship. For although it sounds well to speak of the war as the protest of the North against slavery, the emancipation of the slaves was never intended by the Americans. They then cared for the negroes no more than now, when they would be delighted to carry the whole race to the middle of the Atlantic and sink them there. The North was driven into war, much against its will, by the threats, the insults, and the hostile acts of the South. Abraham Lincoln, in his inaugural address as President, repeated and emphasised his former declaration that " he had no purpose, directly or indirectly, to interfere with the institution of slavery in the States where it existed." And when the war was over and the victory won, he was far too shrewd to desire to admit the negroes to the franchise.   This fatal measure was taken in sheer self-defence to swamp the Southern vote, which would otherwise have restored the intolerable situation previous to the war.   Since that day the miserable negro has been the tool and sport of every party; now petted, now kicked; his strong limbs and feeble brain at the service of any demagogue who might best know how to tickle his vanity and arouse his passions.   If he were other than himself he would be a fit object for compassion; but he is of too low a type to be unhappy, and is probably the only man who laughs to-day in America.

CHAPTER IX.

JUSTICE.

THE administration of justice in the States, on which I have already incidentally remarked, demands some further notice, for it contains the surest test of the measure of freedom enjoyed by a nation. However debased may be the standard of popular morality, and however low the ideal of national duty, that people is still free among whom the judgment seat is pure and unaffected alike by the passion of the mob or the influence of the Government. But, however bravely a people may flaunt its national flag, it is not yet free or has ceased to be so when its judges prostitute their sacred functions ; when they are the hired servants of corrupt and infamous adventurers; when juries are bought and sold ; where the poor are condemned and the rich are criminal with impunity ; and when the outraged people have their ultimate and only refuge from the infamy of the Courts in those parodies of justice which, under the name of Lynch Law, are as much the disgrace of America as the outward sign of its moral decrepitude. That this is the condition of the administration of what is termed justice in many of the States it is impossible to doubt, or that it has accompanied a general depreciation in the standard of public virtue. The contemporary press proclaims it daily in a thousand newspapers, and novelists and essayists are equally frank. Mr. Grant White, who, while an untrustworthy witness on English manners is both a competent and courageous one with regard to America, writes as follows :—

"The deterioration in morals is so certain and so well-known that no one thinks of disputing it. To look through a file of one of our leading newspapers for the last fifteen years is to be led to the conclusion that personal honesty has become the rarest of virtues in the United States, except public probity, which seems no longer to exist. The very ruins of it have disappeared. Our State legislators, instead of being composed of men to whom their constituents looked up, are now composed of men upon whom their constituents look down— not second-rate, nor even third-rate, but fourth- and fifth-rate men, sordid in morals and vulgar in manners, who do politics as a business, for the mere purpose of filling their own pockets. No one thinks of disputing this more than the presence of the blood-sucking insects of summer. Congress itself is openly declared by our own journals to be, because it is known to be, the most corrupt body in civilised Christendom. Within the last fifteen years we have seen men occupying the highest positions in the Government of the United States, who were not only purchasable, but who had been purchased, and at a very small price. I know what I say, and mean it. The Cabinets, during the same period, have been so rotten with corruption that the presence in them of two or three men of integrity could not save them. Worse even than this, judges are openly called Mr. This-one's judge or Mr. That-one's; their owner being generally the controlling stockholder and manager of some great corporation which coins wealth for him and his satellites by schemes of gigantic extortion."

The protest of the American people against this prostitution of justice is Lynch law, which many apologists have attempted to justify on the ground that in new communities, and especially in those which have attracted, in mining districts, an exceptionally brutal, lawless and dangerous class of settlers, the more respectable portion of the community is compelled, in self-defence, and to maintain those elementary principles of society without which an assembly of men is no better than a pack of wolves, to arm themselves with the powers which the law is unable to wield, and punish offenders summarily and severely. This justification is sufficient, and indeed complete so far as those communities are concerned the conditions of which are so primitive that the law is necessarily silent and the social instinct of self-preservation takes its place. But a

L

traveller may go far in America to find circumstances such as these.   Perhaps in towns like
Austin and San Antonio, on the very borderland
of civilisation, lynching may still be a necessary
evil: but in the rudest mining districts of the
Rocky Mountains I have found the general population as orderly as elsewhere.   No doubt if
curiosity or amusement take the traveller into
gambling saloons at midnight in Silverton or
Leadville he will do well to avoid giving offence to
his rough companions ; but the average miner is a
pleasant fellow enough, and there are many quarters
of London, Paris or New York more dangerous to
a well-dressed stranger than the wildest mining
town in the Western States.   Nor is lynching at all
confined to such districts.   Few days pass without
the newspapers recording lynchings in Southern or
Western States, generally with indifference, often
with approval.   In October last, within two or
three days, I noted several such cases which
attracted no particular attention.   In one, in
North Carolina, a negro, in a quarrel with a white
man named Redmond, shot him dead.   Campbell,
the negro, was arrested.   The same night a band of
thirty masked men took him from the jail and
hanged him to a tree, doing their work so quickly,
and it may be supposed so entirely with the

connivance and consent of the jail officials, that
the occurrence was not known till Campbell's body
was found dangling from the tree at daylight.
" Everything" (says ·naively the local newspaper)
" is quiet now." A day or two before, what
the journals call "an effective but unusual
punishment" was inflicted upon a negro of the
name of Lewis Wood, who had been convicted
of outraging a young coloured girl. The mob
waited at the Edgerly station for the train
conveying the prisoner, dragged him a short
distance from the line, chained him to a tree,
covered him with pine knots and chips, and burnt
him to death. About the same day at Lafayette,
Indiana, an old man named Jacob Nell, who had
confessed to the murder of a young girl, Ada
Atkinson, was with difficulty saved from the mob.
The crime seemed to me so motiveless that, in
England, a verdict of acquittal on the ground of
insanity would have been probably given : but the
mob were excited and demanded blood. The
local paper observed calmly that the mob appearing
to have no leader, " it was probable that the law
would be allowed to take its course." Whether
the old maniac was torn to pieces or hung I cannot
say. I did not follow his fortunes further. Such
cases are too common in America to excite more

than a passing interest. The inveterate dislike to the negro on the part of the white population in the Southern States is shown very clearly in these outrages. The assault or the manslaughter committed by a white man is often passed over altogether by the community. The unfortunate negro, whose passions are strong and uncontrolled by education or self-respect, has no such immunity, and is ruthlessly strung up by Judge Lynch, or sometimes, as we have seen, burnt alive.

As these lines are passing through the press, I notice in the American telegraphic intelligence the following announcement :—"A negro who had brutally murdered a woman near Austin, Texas, was chased and captured. He was taken to the scene of the crime by a lynching party of one hundred, and confessed his guilt. He was then roasted to death." The confession extorted under such circumstances was probably worth neither more nor less than those wrung from the victims of the Inquisition previous to an *auto-da-fe*.

"It will be noticed," writes the New York *Tribune*, "that the privilege of becoming furious because one of their race has been killed by one of the other is strictly reserved to the whites. The negroes are expected to be serene, if not grateful, when negroes are killed by whites."

The conviction of eight "sturdy farmer boys" in Georgia for outrages on negroes was received with

general surprise, the more so when it appeared that
a majority of the jury was composed of whites, it
having been found impossible to punish such
offences which were justified by the sentiment of
the white community, and verdicts of acquittal were
always returned. The evidence in this case showed
that the prisoners had whipped, shot, and otherwise
maltreated negroes who had voted for Mr. Speer,
the independent Democratic candidate for Congress.
One negro swore to having received one hundred
and seventy-five lashes, on the ground that he was
a " d——d Speer negro," besides being struck with
steel knuckles, kicked, and threatened with death.
Another had been shot in three places. The
defence was a general *alibi*, but the witnesses
positively identified several of the defendants; and
the secret of the verdict probably was that the
evidence was too strong to be safely disregarded
by even a sympathising jury.

The following incident, which occurred in August
last in the same State, will show the manner in
which the negro can be treated by "a member of
a good family ":—

"While Mrs. George W. Felts was shaking fruit from a
tree, Peter Broomfield, coloured, asked her to be careful that
she did not break off any branches. Mrs. Felts lost her
temper and complained to her husband of what Broomfield
had said. Yesterday, while the latter was at work roofing a

house, in company with three other men, Felts appeared at
the foot of the ladder with a double-barrelled shotgun. Broomfield comprehended the situation and pleaded for mercy.
Felts said, ' If you will come down and let me flog you, that
will be the end of it ; if you don't I will kill you.' Broomfield's
terrified companions urged him to take the flogging and save
his life.   As Broomfield commenced a descent of the ladder,
Felts, without saying a word, fired both barrels of the gun
and two balls from a revolver into the coloured man's body,
and he fell to the ground a corpse.   Felts then walked to
where the body lay, and with an oath fired three bullets from
his pistol into the dead man's breast.   Then, turning to the
terrified spectators, Felts said, ' There, I guess that fixed
him !' and walked away, since which he has not been seen.
The negroes are greatly excited, and say if they can capture
Felts they will burn him alive in the woods.   Felts is twenty-
seven years old and a member of a good family."

If it should be said that from an outrage such as
this, committed by a passionate man, no argument
can be drawn, I would only reply that the incident
may be taken for what it is worth, and derives its
only significance from the general surprise with
which the Ku-Klux convictions above referred to
were received.

The *Echo*, which is the greatest admirer of
American institutions in the London press, and
which has criticised my opinions of the Harvest of
Democracy with some asperity, lately observed in
its leading columns that it was remarkable that
American public opinion seldom made a mistake
in its judgment of a criminal, whatever the courts

might do, and that there was no case on record of
a man having been lynched on evidence that would
not have procured his conviction in any well-
constituted and honest court. A more laughable
statement was surely never framed. It is
obviously impossible to be certain of the guilt of
a man who has been hanged or burnt alive before
trial. It is as obviously unreasonable to insist on
the guilt of an unfortunate who has been lynched
after an acquittal in open court. Yet such cases
form a considerable proportion of these outrages.
Nor do the Americans themselves adopt the
illogical view of their English apologist. The
Century of April last writes as follows :—

"It cannot be too often nor too strongly proclaimed that
these lynchings themselves are crimes ; that they are utterly
without excuse ; that they furnish a remedy which is worse
than the disease. When a score of men can find no better way
of expressing their detestation of murder than by becoming
murderers themselves, our civilisation seems to have reduced
itself to an absurdity. Moreover, lynch law is not much more
accurate in its measurement and dispensation of justice than
the lax administration against which it protests. The mob
is neither judicial nor chivalrous ; the weak and defenceless
are far more likely to suffer at its hands than the strong and
prosperous, as is shown by the fact that the victims of more
than half the lynchings reported last year were Southern
negroes.

"Nevertheless, the failure of criminal justice, which makes
room for mobs and lynching, is a greater disgrace than the
savagery of the mobs. The fact that thirteen out of fourteen

murderers escape the gallows is the one damning fact that blackens the record of our criminal jurisprudence.   No American ought to indulge in any boasting about his native land, while the evidence remains that the laws made for the protection of human life are thus shamelessly trampled under foot.   No occupant of the bench and no member of the bar ought to rest until those monstrous abuses which result in the utter defeat of justice are thoroughly corrected."

The statistics of criminal justice in the States to which the *Century* refers show that, during the year 1882, twelve hundred and sixty-six murders were reported ; and in 1883, no less than fifteen hundred and seventeen—a proportion three times as large as in England, and nearly double that of those European countries where crimes of violence are most common and least regarded.   Against this black record there stand only ninety-three legal executions ; so that the deterrent influence of the death penalty, where only one murderer in fifteen meets his deserts, can hardly be considered very great.   Where the law has thus grievously and conspicuously failed, the wild and blind passion of the mob has pretended to supply its deficiencies, and the same year records no less than one hundred and eighteen lynchings.

The weakness of the law and its corrupt and inefficient administration are the direct cause of this state of things.   But, as the *Century* truly observes, the remedy is worse than the disease. Justice is brought into contempt both by the usurpation of its functions by the mob and by its own cowardice and venality. How many persons, it might reasonably be asked, were judicially punished during the year 1883 for their participation in these 118 mob murders. It is notorious that the law is ordinarily powerless to punish such outrages; while it is equally certain that their effect upon the people is of the most demoralising kind.

Last September I was in Cheyenne, Wyoming, a day or two after a lynching had occurred, and I inquired into its circumstances from some of the townsmen who had assisted at the ceremony. So far as I remember, the victim was accused of having murdered a man whom he had met camping in the prairie, who had invited him to share his meal, and whom, when sleeping, he killed and robbed. The crime was an atrocious one, though whether the accused were guilty can be never known, for, having been arrested, he was lodged in the lockup, whence the good citizens, fearing that he might escape punishment, through the uncertainty of the law, incontinently took him, without any resistance on the part of the officials, and hanged him to a telegraph pole in the principal street. One of my informants was a young man employed in a large dry-goods store, who assured me that, although he took his gun, he only attended the execution in the character of a spectator.   The self-constituted judges and executioners were, he said, the most respectable inhabitants of the town, shopkeepers and merchants.   The hangman was a telephone clerk, and as, mounted on a ladder, he drew the rope, already round the victim's neck, to the top of the pole, he put the end to his ear and shouted "Hullo," in telephonic fashion, attracting the attention of the person at the other end of the line.   This brutal witticism was received with great laughter by the crowd, though it may have been less appreciated by the condemned, who was straightway launched into eternity.   No one of the Cheyenne people to whom I spoke seemed in any way ashamed of the occurrence.   The murderer, they said, would have escaped punishment if he had been sent for trial, and their procedure, if less regular, was more certain and just than that of the courts.   Now we may allow, for the sake of argument, that this hanged man was guilty, though of this there can exist no legal proof; and, further, that his execution was due to the fear that, if regularly tried, he would escape proper punishment.   Yet to a person who has been privileged to live in a civilised country, where the passions of

the mob are held in control by the firm and
impartial administration of the law, the respectable
citizens of Cheyenne, which is a wealthy, prosperous
town, with churches, banks, hotels, and daily newspapers, seem little removed from savages. If the
people of Wyoming or any other State desire a
pure administration of justice, they can obtain it.
The remedy is in their own hands. The judges
are not appointed by the Government, but elected
by themselves: the juries who acquit murderers
are their own friends and comrades, and the
defeat of justice is due to their own low standard
of public morality.

If an illustration, on a larger scale, of the mal-
administration of justice and the demoralisation
which results from the practice of lynching be
required, the recent riots at Cincinnati furnish it.
The details are too notorious to need lengthy
repetition. Suffice it to say that a sentence of
twenty years' imprisonment having been passed on
a young man named Berner for the murder and
robbery of his employer, general indignation was
excited in the town. The people had long complained that murderers were habitually acquitted,
admitted to bail, or sentenced to inadequate terms
of imprisonment, and they believed that any
criminal might escape whose friends were in a

position to fee unscrupulous lawyers to bribe equally unscrupulous juries. A mass meeting was held, which, speedily losing self-control, started for the jail with the declared intention of lynching the murderers confined there. The attack on the building was repulsed by the police and militia, with a loss to the mob of some sixty-five killed and wounded. The excitement continually rose higher : for two days the fighting lasted. Troops were poured into the town, and a Gatling gun was used with terrible effect on the rioters. At the conclusion of the affray, some two hundred were killed and wounded, and the Court House, which had cost a quarter of a million of dollars, was in ashes. Some four thousand soldiers were encamped in the streets, and Cincinnati resembled a city taken by assault.

I can imagine a simple German emigrant, on his arrival in New York, reading the dark story of the Cincinnati riots with a feeling akin to stupefaction. Was it then for this that he had left Bismarck and the tyranny of the Old World behind ? Was this the America of his dreams, where the rich were beneficent, the poor content, and where every free-man enjoyed his own in honourable independence ? Instead of the paradise he had imagined, he found a pandemonium, with the people in revolt against the law ; the troops mowing down the mob with machine guns, and Liberty, her eyes alight with unholy passions and her shining garments all be-smirched with blood, hounding on her worshippers to arson, pillage, and murder. How could the simple Teuton understand that this was the result of government of the people for the people, or that the American judge would not only, like Pilate, have condemned the blameless victim and released Barabbas, but, with a deeper infamy, would have divided with Judas the price of blood ?

If we could believe that the Cincinnati riots signified no more than a genuine protest of respect-able citizens against the systematic prostitution of justice, the friends of America and of freedom might regard them with equanimity, if not approval. Desperate diseases need desperate remedies and in politics, as in war, omelettes are not to be made without breaking eggs. But I do not believe that this view of the case would be correct. The riots of Cincinnati were less due to the indignation of the people at any inadequate sentence—for, in every country, such failures of justice are common from the tenderness of the judge or the humanitarian sentiment of the jury, than to the general demorali-sation of the popular conscience due to the habitual and unpunished practice of extra-judicial murder under the name of lynch law. To the mob a

lynching has all the savage delight and attraction
which Imperial Rome found in gladiatorial exhibitions.   The murder which caused this particular
outbreak was by no means an atrocious one, and
was brought home to the murderer by his voluntary
surrender and confession.   It was punished by a
sentence of twenty years' imprisonment, only less
severe than death, and by many would be held to
be far worse than the death penalty.   But a certain
number of citizens were determined that their
opinion of the appropriate punishment should,
according to Judge Lynch's arbitrary procedure,
over-ride the decision of the court ; and they were
surprised and indignant that the jail officials did
not fail in their duty and surrender the destined
victims after the usual and decent amount of coy
resistance.   The passions of the mob were soon
aroused : the tiger had tasted blood ; and the pretended purifiers of the judgment seat were speedily
reinforced by the large contingent of brutality and
crime which is to be found in the slums of every
considerable city.   The contest was then between
order and anarchy ; and the troops were as justified
in firing on the rioters as was the Republican
Government of France in suppressing the Commune
in a similar manner.   The character of the riot is
clearly shown in the savage attack made by the

mob on the men engaged in extinguishing the fire
in a shop which was being pillaged, one fireman
being killed and several wounded. What does
American Liberty say to these poor victims,
wounded and slain by their fellow-citizens while
discharging a dangerous and honourable duty?
This is not the blood which cements the altar of
Freedom, but rather that with which African
savages besmear their cruel idols. If there be a
page in human history which, more than another,
might give occasion for sorrow to angels and
laughter to devils, it is surely the story of the
Cincinnati riots.

Although lynch law, both in the inequity of its
procedure and in the moral lassitude which it
induces, is the most startling symptom of judicial
maladministration, there are many concurrent signs
of the decadence of the respect due to law and of
the paralysis of its healthy action. The criminal
law is as little respected as feared, and, out of the
morbid sentimentalism of judges and juries and
the love of excitement in the people, who are disposed to consider every one a hero who can sufficiently amuse them, has arisen a race of lawyers
and experts who can prolong a trial till a jury
acquits because it has forgotten the evidence, and
who can successfully maintain that the most cold-

blooded and deliberate murder was but the result of a pardonable hallucination. English procedure can show many lengthy trials, and the famous Tichborne case was discreditable to our courts ; but the point in dispute was obscure and of absorbing interest ; while the outrageous conduct of the counsel for the defence was universally reprobated by the profession to which he belonged. But we have nothing to compare with the scandal of the Star Route case, the second trial of which lasted six months, and ended in a gross miscarriage of justice ; or the indecency of the Guiteau case, where the assassin of the President was permitted, for months, to browbeat and insult judges and counsel alike, while his blasphemy and insolence were applauded by a public as noisy and disrespectful as the gallery of a suburban theatre. The comments of the *New York Herald* on the Cincinnati riots are significant enough :

"What with facile coroners and criminal authorities who are chosen for political reasons and obey the nod of a boss, and the plea of insanity and all the dilatory processes of the land, the murderer who gets hanged at last is an unusually unlucky mortal. But while we do not see any probability that our citizens are likely to try the Cincinnati remedy against this evil, yet if they should be disposed that way, they may well remember the troublesome elements that smoulder just beneath the peaceful surface of city life. We have a society here that meets every Sunday night to hear speeches in favour of universal murder with dynamite. We have a colony of the men who tried to burn the city of Paris. We have Most and Schwab and an army of their adherents. We have perhaps a hundred thousand men who would contemplate the burning of this city as a noble sacrifice on the altar of their principles."

No critic of American institutions can, with justice or honesty, refuse to make the fullest allowance for the heterogeneity of the American population, and the enormous difficulties caused by the swarm of immigrants who pour into New York at the rate of a thousand a day from every part of Europe. But in drawing from American difficulties the lesson for English guidance, we cannot forget that the root of the evil lies in universal suffrage, untempered by any educational or moral checks, and in opening the ballot to all but the Chinese (who would probably vote far more reasonably than a large number of more favoured citizens), thus taking the power from those who could use it aright, and intrusting it to those who have no knowledge to use it wisely, even had they the wish to do so. The law then becomes, as we have seen, the accomplice of the criminal; and the orderly majority are thrust into the position so abhorrent to a civilised community, of holding their own by force of arms. Nothing can be more hardening to the national conscience than this attitude. An

M

American friend, writing to me from New York on
the subject of the low Irish in that city, says :—

"They are clamorous and noisy, and, like O'Donovan
Rossa, make a great noise to convince people of what they
call their power. When they become lawless, however, we
shoot them down, and shall continue to do so."

Drastic remedies such as these, inevitable as
they may be, are not to be prescribed with a light
heart. They seem to signify the negation of law ;
and the more prosaic procedure of the English
courts, even when administering the odious neces-
sity of a Coercion Act, is more in accord with
nineteenth-century civilisation.

CHAPTER X.

THE COST OF DEMOCRACY.

THE cheapness of democratic institutions is the ground on which they have been most frequently recommended to popular approval. Demagogues have pointed the attention of the mob to the long Civil Lists of princes, and to the pensions and fat offices which a privileged aristocracy have divided among their order ; and have contrasted this system of jobbery with the chaste republican simplicity which, instead of the imperial ermine, is content to be clothed with virtue and public spirit. It is then necessary to examine these high pretensions. History is full of the extravagance of Courts, and in no country more than our own has titled incompetence drained the public purse, and brought confusion on our policy at home and abroad. Would the adoption of republicanism abolish these evils, which, in a purer atmosphere, and in the light of a fuller publicity, have grown daily less conspicuous ?

In France the new Republic has cost twice as much as the Empire ; and the expenditure shows no sign of having reached its highest point. But it is not possible here to examine the statistics of the French Republic, and we will be content with a few of those connected with military and naval administration in the United States. First, it is necessary to understand the duties which are expected of the American army. Its services are not likely to be required against a foreign enemy, and it is thus maintained for home service in such numbers and efficiency as may enable it to preserve order in any exceptional emergencies, such as the riots of Cincinnati or Pittsburg, to guard the Mexican frontier, and to restrain the raids of Indian tribes. The last duty is that upon which it is mostly engaged, and a most unsatisfactory duty it is. The world may judge of the value which a republic sets on liberty when it studies the treatment of the negroes before the war, and the Indians to-day, at the hands of the people and Government of the United States. If all the Indian tribes—men, women, and children through-out the States and Territories—be enumerated they amount to some 66,000 souls, the population of a second-rate town. Yet a long series of Indian outrages and reprisals have and are taking place, which a nation of 50,000,000 does not disdain to call "Indian wars." The true origin of the disputes is in the weakness of the executive and the popular contempt for the law. The squatters and settlers of the West look upon the Indians as "vermin," to be exterminated as speedily as possible. The miserable savages have no refuge save in the generosity and justice of the Government, which has set apart for their especial use and benefit reservations within which no white settlements are permitted. But they are harassed and persecuted on every side; their undoubted rights are disallowed or confiscated, and corrupt place-hunters, ignorant of their language and customs, are appointed to superintend their delicate relations with their white neighbours. Only the other day one of these officials, Mr. Commissioner Price, took upon himself to abolish polygamy. The usage was universal and immemorial in all the tribes, but did not commend itself to the enlightened views of Mr. Price, who not only proposed to forbid it in the future, but to insist upon all those Indians who had two or more wives summarily discarding all but the one he considered permissible. As I have not heard of

a new "Indian war" I presume that Mr. Price
has been extinguished by some superior official
possessed of more intelligence; but the incident,
extraordinary as it may appear, is a fair illustration
of the policy of the Indian Bureau. It is impossible not to sympathise with the sentiment
of disgust and contempt with which the shrewd,
hard-working Yankee regards the dirty, lazy, and
irreclaimable savage whose lands and hunting-
grounds he considers his lawful spoil. The Indian
of romance, as drawn by Fenimore Cooper, who
seems in life and manners to have been as much
of a savage as his favourite models, is hardly
recognisable in the squalid and repulsive outcasts
one meets in New Mexico and other by-paths of
American civilisation. The Indian refuses to work
in any way or for any consideration, and subsists
on the chase and on the weekly dole of flour
which he is by no means too proud to accept from
the Government. If he cannot dig, to beg he is
by no means ashamed. It is obvious that the
sooner he dies out and makes room for more
useful persons the better; yet this does not, from
an administrative point of view, excuse the
Government for the unworthy and dishonest policy
which they have permitted towards those who are
so few and weak that they should not look to the

authorities for protection in vain. In British India there are many aboriginal races, like Bhils and Gonds, who are of no account as a source of revenue or strength, yet the Government takes fully as much care of their interests as if they were a rich and civilised community. In Canada, where the Indians are numerous, we have no record of constant Indian wars, and the white and coloured races live side by side orderly and peacefully. The difference is due to the care with which complaints are investigated and grievances redressed, while Indian affairs are conducted by officials who understand the business, instead of by the first adventurer who can bribe the wire-pullers of Washington to give him office.

Although the duties to be performed by the United States army are few, and would be nominal were the Indian Bureau administered with ordinary honesty and discretion, it must not be imagined that its cost is at all proportional to its work or numbers. In 1881, the war expenditure, in a time of profound peace, was \$40,500,000 ; and the number of regular troops was 20,000. For $1\frac{1}{4}$ larger expenditure, Germany maintains, on a peace footing, 419,659 men : for an expenditure $1\frac{1}{2}$ greater, France maintains 470,600 men, and England, whose

military expenditure is, from obvious reasons,
exceptionally heavy, for § greater expenditure
maintains (exclusive of India) 133,720 men.

For Englishmen, and especially for those who
look ignorantly and blindly across the Atlantic to
the great Republic of the West, and who, in their
simplicity, imagine that the adoption of republican
institutions would make the burthen of life in
England less heavy, there can be no more wholesome course of study than the financial statistics of
the United States during the present century.   I
will attempt, most briefly, to explain their general
features so far as military and naval expenditure is
concerned, in order that the cost of democracy may
be fairly realised.

The year 1801 found the young Republic at
peace, under the Presidency of Thomas Jefferson.
The strength of the regular army, as fixed by
Congress, was 5,144, and the cost $1,672,000.   The
expenditure declined for some years, and the war
with England then raised it to an average of
$16,000,000 during the years 1812 to 1816.   It fell
to one half of this the following year ; to $2,500,000
in   1820 ;   and   fluctuated   from $3,000,000 to
$6,000,000 until the year 1836, when it suddenly
rose to $12,000,000, at which point it remained till
1839, when stringent and successful efforts at reduc-

tion were made, expenditure falling to $9,000,000 in 1839, and to $3,000,000 in 1843. With the year 1845, the first and economical period of war expenditure ceased for America; and the second phase commenced with war with Mexico and the annexation of Texas, and an annual expenditure which between 1846 to 1860 averaged $17,000,000. The period 1862 to 1866 must be excluded from the calculation, as the enormous cost of the civil war would make the statistics of normal expenditure valueless.

In 1867, the military expenditure on peace establishments was $95,250,000, and it was not till 1871 that the effect of the war no longer appeared directly in the estimates. The charges were then some $35,750,000, and they have averaged $40,000,000 during the present decade.

The naval expenditure must now be considered. This, in 1801, was considerably larger than that on the army, and amounted to $2,111,424. It was however, kept below this sum until 1812, when war being declared with Great Britain, the cost of the navy at once doubled. But at no period of the war, in which the American navy was most distinguished for gallantry and enterprise, did the expenditure exceed $8,500,000. This was in 1815. With the conclusion of peace the naval budget fell to $4,000,000 ; during the period 1817 to 1846 it fluctuated between $3,000,000 and $6,000,000. The second phase of naval as of military finance then set in. From 1846 till the civil war, some $12,000,000 were spent annually on the navy; the year succeeding the civil war, 1867, found the expenditure $31,000,000 ; in 1874, it was the same, and the last year, 1881, for which we have figures, the naval expenditure was $15,686,671.

These results may be best thrown into the tabular statement on p. 171, showing the expenditure at different periods of the history of the past century on both the army and navy, and the number of troops maintained at the several dates. For convenience the sums are given in thousands of dollars, smaller sums being omitted.

However dull statistics may ordinarily be, no one can deny that these figures are both instructive and amusing. Many curious financial phenomena may be discovered within them. It will be observed that while in the year 1850, 10,000 men of the regular army cost $9,000,000 annually, they could not be procured in 1881 for less than $20,000,000 ; that reduction in the number of the troops signifies an increase in the total expenditure on the army, and that 20,000 men cost more, by many millions, than 27,000, or than 35,000. In

return for this enormous annual expenditure on
the army there are 20,000 men on paper. Whether

Year.	Army.	Navy.	Regular Army.	Remarks.
1801	1,672,000	2,111,000	5,144	War with England.
1812	11,817,000	3,957,000	11,831	
1815	14,794,000	8,660,000	9,413	
1817	8,004,000	3,314,000	9,980	
1827	3,948,000	4,263,000	6,184	
1835	5,759,000	3,864,000	7,198	
1837	13,682,000	6,646,000	Do.	
1839	8,916,000	6,182,000	12,539	Florida War.
1843	2,908,000	3,727,000	8,613	
1847	35,840,000	7,900,000	17,812	Mexican War.
1850	9,687,000	7,904,000	10,320	
1855	14,648,000	13,327,000	Do.	
1859	23,154,000	14,690,000	12,931	Peace Establishment.
1860	16,472,000	11,514,000	Do.	
1861	23,000,000	12,387,000	Do.	
1862—66	—	—	—	Civil War.
1867	95,224,000	31,034,000	54,641	Peace Establishment.
1868	123,246,000	25,775,000	52,922	
1869	78,501,000	20,000,000	Do.	
1870	57,655,000	21,780,000	37,313	
1871	35,799,000	19,431,000	35,353	
1872	35,372,000	21,249,000	32,264	
1873	46,323,000	23,526,000	Do.	
1874	42,313,000	30,932,000	Do.	
1875	41,120,000	21,497,000	27,489	
1876	38,070,000	18,963,000	Do.	
1877	37,082,000	14,959,000	Do.	
1878	32,154,000	17,365,000	Do.	
1879	40,425,000	15,125,000	20,000	
1880	38,116,000	13,536,000	Do.	
1881	40,466,000	15,686,000	Do.	

they really exist or not is unknown, and I have
never met any one who has seen them. They are
supposed to be quartered in remote districts of

New Mexico, Indian Territory, and Arizona, where they probably are the only inhabitants, and where, at any rate, there are no critics to count their numbers on parade.

Before leaving military expenditure, there is another item to which I would invite the attention of English Radicals and the editor of the *Financial Reform Almanack*. This is Pensions. In 1861, the charge for pensions was $1,034,000; in 1862, $852,000. At the close of the war, 1867, it had risen to $21,000,000; in 1868, to $23,750,000; in 1871, to $34,500,000; in 1878, it had fallen to $27,000,000; in 1879, it again rose to $35,000,000; in 1880, it reached the prodigious total of $56,750,000; and in 1881 it again sank to $50,000,000, exceeding by $10,000,000 the total expenditure on the army. The physiological phenomenon which these figures present is startling enough. At the close of a war, and when the distribution of pensions has been once made, the Treasury would expect the ordinary laws of mortality to reduce annually the pension charges. But the veterans of the civil war appear to renew their strength like the eagles. Not content with immortality themselves, they have the power of dividing and multiplying their individuality like zoophytes; and, unless some check on their power of reduplication be discovered, these honest warriors will, in twenty years, absorb the whole revenue of the United States.

The expenditure which falls under the head of Indians is remarkable. These interesting savages cost President Jefferson $31.22c. in the year 1800 It was not till thirty years later that their charges had reached $1,000,000 annually. Like the army, and unlike the pensioners, their numbers have been continually decreasing, and, as above noted, they only number at the present time 66,407 souls. Yet, like the army and the veterans, their cost constantly increases. For the decade preceding the war, they cost some $3,000,000 annually. They now cost $6,000,000, and a few years ago they cost between $8,000,000 and $9,000,000. Every Indian family should thus receive from the benevolent Government about $500 a year, for no "Indian war" expenditure is excluded in the item now under discussion. Perhaps if it be roughly estimated that of the $56,500,000 which are annually paid under the head of pensions and Indians, $40,000,000 represent unblushing robbery from the United States Treasury, we shall be well within the truth. At least half of the $40,000,000 of war expenditure may be assumed to disappear in a similar fashion.

In the year 1814, when the young Republic disputed, not without glory, the dominion of the sea with the powerful British Empire, its navy cost one-half of what it does to-day. Its peace expenditure was, in 1818, some $2,000,000 or $3,000,000, compared with the $15,000,000 which is now wasted on a navy which has neither ships nor guns. Admiral D. Porter, and other authorities as respectable, declare that the American navy consists of officers and water without any ships. It is true that the protective tariff has annihilated the merchant shipping, so that the navy is no longer required to protect American commerce abroad, but its naval weakness is unworthy the dignity of a great country. It is certainly not for the advantage of England that America should adopt free trade and again cover the sea with merchant ships, but the day will probably come when the farmers of the West and the artisans of the East will unite in refusing to pay double prices for almost every necessary of life in order to swell the profits of the manufacturers. But under a Republic, where the minority rule and the majority suffer, the hour of deliverance may be far distant. In the meantime, the United States can, as a naval power, be hardly reckoned in the third rank. Congress appears to have awakened to the fact that this state of things

is discreditable, and extra grants of large amounts
are now being proposed to increase the navy.   But
a creeping paralysis has attacked the Executive, and
Congress votes money in vain.   Three and a half
millions of dollars have been passed for building
four steel cruisers, one of which, the *Dolphin*, is
almost complete.   But experts declare the type an
inferior one ; the engines are unsuited to the ships,
and there is no authority with power to prevent a
barren experiment being indefinitely repeated.
Since the close of the civil war, some $385,000,000
have been spent upon the navy, more than it
cost from the foundation of the Republic to
1860, when it was able to make itself everywhere
respected.   This money might, as Congress has
itself declared, have been as profitably thrown
into the sea.

Can it be matter for surprise that, having regard
to the profligate expenditure of the past, Mr.
Randall and the Democratic party he leads in Congress are opposing the proposed grants to the navy,
and would even refuse to complete the monitors
without which the ports are defenceless, or to
purchase the guns without which the new steel
cruisers cannot put to sea.

Such is the cost of Democracy.   Up to the date
of the civil war, some decency was observed in the

public expenditure. The result of that unfortunate struggle was like a typhoid fever, which alters the whole constitution of the sufferer, and not unfrequently results in rapid consumption. The resources of the United States are too vast, and the people too energetic, for the one to be speedily exhausted or for the other to be vitally affected. But the rapid consumption has set in, and has first attacked the Treasury. The reckless extravagance and robbery of the war demoralised the entire community. The people discovered how easy it was to rob the national exchequer, and every one hastened to become rich at the public expense. The highest officials seem powerless to stem the torrent of corruption. Few of them attempt to do so. They recall the Cornish parson of Peter Pindar's poem, who was preaching when the cry, " A wreck, a wreck !" was heard without the church. For a moment he attempted vainly to restrain his congregation, but, finding them beyond control—

> " ' Stop, stop,' cried he, ' at least one prayer :
> Let me get down, and all start fair.' "

CHAPTER XI.

FOREIGN POLICY.

IT has been seen, in the last chapter, that the United States are in no position to take an active part in foreign policy, even should they be disposed to do so. Their army, costly though it be, is only sufficient for home requirements; while the navy could not meet on equal terms that of a fourth-rate European power. But of the latent power of America there can be no doubt : and its attitude is so different from that of the French Republic, whose restlessness and insolent aggression in every quarter of the world is inconveniently conspicuous, that it would be interesting to inquire whether apathy or truculence were the normal effect of republican institutions. Especially is such an inquiry interesting and important for England with her tangle of foreign relations, and she cannot wisely adopt American

N

institutions without determining what effect they would have on her foreign policy.

We have the most exact descriptions in history of the sentiments and conditions of the fighting republics of Athens, Sparta, Florence, and Venice ; and we must allow its due importance to the fiery enthusiasm which carried France triumphantly through Europe at the close of the last century. But the more attentively these instances are regarded, the more probable does it appear that the fierce and aggressive spirit which animated the policy of the Greek and Italian republics was rather oligarchical and aristocratic than democratic in the modern sense of the word. This was certainly the case with Italy ; and although it cannot be denied that in the little wild-cat republic of Athens every freeman had as much opportunity of voting and talking as if he had been a member of the British Parliament, yet the prevailing temper was aristocratic, as was inevitable where a minority of freemen rule a majority of slaves. As for France, the excitability and restlessness of her people are such as to make her an unsafe illustration of normal political phenomena ; yet it may be asserted that, while the new-born republican fury had its undoubted effect during the early days of the Revolution, chiefly stirred to action by the unwarrantable attempt of the European monarchs to crush a movement the success of which might endanger their own stability, the victories of France were mostly won under the Napoleonic despotism. The danger to the world from French republicanism chiefly arises from the enormous proportion of vanity in the character of the people, demanding in the national policy constant gratification. It is a jealous deity destroying those who do not burn incense on its altar. Consequently, Republican France, directed by statesmen whose ephemeral existence depends on popular caprice, is more likely to be aggressive in her foreign policy than when controlled by a ruler who can sit careless above the thunder of the mob. Even he is never safe. The French tiger devours his tamer the moment he makes a mistake in the performance ; as Napoleon III. discovered to his cost. England has never tried a republic ; for the experiment between 1650 and 1660 was a strict military despotism barely veiled by constitutionalism. To-day the English are more democratic than of old, in that the people have a larger voice in the national policy ; but it is difficult to say that the country is less loyal, less conservative, or less disposed to fight for a reasonable, or, indeed, an unreasonable, cause. If public

utterances were to be regarded, it might seem that
the Tory party were more in favour of a bold and
active foreign policy than the Liberals ; but this
is extremely questionable, and in opposition to it
is the fact that among the Liberals themselves,
putting aside certain eccentric members of Parliament who in no way represent the national
feeling, the advanced Left is far more thorough,
aggressive, and imperialistic in matters of foreign
policy than the moderate Liberals or Whigs, who
would seem to have adopted the policy of
quieta non movere.

If the case of America be now considered it will
be seen that her epoch of aggressiveness in foreign
policy was while she was practically governed by
an aristocratic oligarchy.   This was previous to the
war, when the slave owners of the South dominated
the political situation ; and they might have retained
their supremacy till to-day, so weak and spiritless
was the Northern majority, had they not, in sheer
wantonness, bullied the North into the war which
naturally ended in their own destruction.   In those
days the United States were certainly accustomed
to bounce and bluster a good deal ; but, endeavouring
to look at their political action with impartial eyes,
it had about it an air of patriotism and genuine
national spirit which is less conspicuous under a

more popular administration.   It is true that the
war, with all its demoralisation, had a tranquilizing
effect upon the American temper.   The people felt
that they had at last done a very big thing.   They
had killed and wounded as many men as would
have satisfied Cæsar or Napoleon, and had spent
on the ennobling operation some six thousand
eight hundred millions of dollars.   It mattered
little whether the half a million of men who had
been killed in battle or who died of wounds or
disease knew for what they had been fighting ; or
whether the money had, for the most part, gone
into the pockets of thieves and swindlers who built
their fortunes on the calamity of the nation.   The
Americans had fairly bought, in fire and blood, the
right to hold up their heads among the down-trodden
peoples of the Old World.   Like them, they had
been driven to battle and death for the lying schemes
of shifty adventurers ; like them, they were heavily
taxed in order that saloon keepers and shoddy
contractors might cover their vulgar wives and
daughters with diamonds.   If such glorious results
do not consolidate and dignify a nation, the
political theories of England and Europe must
be mistaken.

The Monroe doctrine which was, previous to the
war, the most generally accepted exposition of

American foreign policy, as stated by its founder in his seventh annual message, in December, 1823, was a wise and reasonable declaration of policy. It was directly aimed at Spain and Portugal, whose colonial policy is, and ever has been, obnoxious to all liberal and enlightened principles, and warned them that the great Republic of the West would not tolerate their continued efforts to re-conquer those South American countries which had, most happily, escaped from their rapacious clutches. Further, the President of the United States categorically informed those Powers that his Government would consider any attempt on their part to extend their system to any portion of the Western Hemisphere as dangerous to the peace and safety of the United States. The policy thus enunciated was as successful as it was wise, and Englishmen who condemn it may be sure that any British Government, under similar circumstances, would not only have done as much, but more, for Cuba and Hayti would long ago have been annexed to the Empire. England would not wish the Monroe doctrine to be used, as has sometimes been attempted by too zealous Secretaries of State at Washington, against herself, and this is natural enough. Nor was the Monroe doctrine so designed ; and the most ardent Republican could not pretend that freedom and civilisation were in danger from the extension of the political influence of England. The doctrine is one which the two branches of the Anglo-Saxon race would do well to preserve and fortify rather than contemn and deny. The British States of Australia, which a wise statesmanship would cease to term or treat as colonies, have lately proclaimed the same principle for the South Pacific, with the full and cordial approval of the majority of their fellow-countrymen in England. It is not a paltry question of the transportation to New Caledonia of a few thousand French convicts that is at issue : this the Australians could easily settle for themselves; it is the claim, which will yearly be more loudly pressed, that the whole of the South Pacific has fallen by fortune to the Anglo-Saxon race, which alone has the power to hold and civilise it—and that other nations who choose to dispute this claim must do so by force of arms.

The Monroe doctrine, as originally designed, was explained by Mr. President Adams in 1826. He desired to summon a Congress of American States, who should agree to take independent measures against the establishment of any future European colony within their borders, and thus secure and develop the freedom of the new and struggling Republics of South America, with which the United

States were naturally in strong sympathy. This authoritative declaration of what the Monroe doctrine really was, by a member of President Monroe's Cabinet, differed very materially from its later and more aggressive development, binding the United States to resist all colonisation or interference by any European Power within the New World. The idea of the founders of the doctrine was evidently to strengthen the hands of the Southern Republics, and to invite each State in North or South America to take steps to protect itself from foreign intrusion. But the intention of a formula which has been altogether changed in practical application has little beyond historical interest ; and the Monroe doctrine in any shape has fallen out of fashion. It was lately dragged forth by Mr. Secretary Blaine to frighten the promoters of the Panama Canal scheme, but was not very effective, and was relegated to obscurity. So little does the passion for foreign annexation now animate Americans, that the occupation of the Sandwich Islands by England or Germany would not form the subject of remonstrance, though it was once a burning question ; and were these islands offered to the United States as a free gift, it is doubtful whether they would be accepted by Congress.

There is in the foreign policy of America nothing unfriendly to England. The good feeling between the two countries is fortunately increasing year by year, and so long as the States confine their attention exclusively to the American continent our interests are not likely to clash. Canada is not a source of anxiety; for while, on the one hand, this dependency is exceedingly loyal to the Crown, there is, on the other, no desire on the part of the States to absorb it. Should a policy of annexation, contrary to the wish of the Dominion, be ever launched, England and Canada will be quite able to take care of themselves.

The large and rapidly increasing German population of the States may have a tranquillising effect on American relations with England, and to some extent neutralise the Irish element ; for there can be little doubt that English sentiment is tending towards the natural alliance with Germany as opposed to France, who, since she has adopted republican institutions, has proved herself worthless as an ally. We can have no true sympathy with France, whose attitude towards us is uniformly unfriendly, and whose interests are opposed to ours in every quarter of the world ; while with Germany we have the bond of a common origin, creed, and interests.

The sentimental regard for the Russian Government, which was once so strongly and frequently expressed in America, has died out. It was always an unnatural and artificial growth, and had its origin in the astuteness of Russia attempting to make political capital out of the mistakes of the upper classes in England, who, for reasons which need not here be discussed, gave their sympathy and moral support to the Southern Democrats in the civil war. Russia, who foresaw the inevitable result of the struggle, sided warmly with the North, and earned a cheap gratitude, which for some time made an imposing display. But the farce was played out with the return of cordiality between England and America, for it was impossible that either of these nations should long regard with any other sentiment than disgust the domestic policy of Russia. It was an evil day for the Liberal party in England when fortune compelled it to appear as the advocate of Russian fraud and aggression in south-eastern Europe, to champion a Power whose hostility to England is deep-seated and inveterate, and whose political methods are abhorrent to every sentiment of Liberalism. America and England have both fallen into the same snare, and we may hope that for them, at least, the fowler may in future spread his nets in vain.

Great as the evils of the political system in America may be, and serious as are the dangers which lie before the Republic, the people are far too energetic and high-spirited to view them with any unworthy alarm. The pride in the greatness and wealth of their country which is felt and expressed by Americans, their confidence in its future, and the equanimity with which they regard the dangers or troubles of the hour, are admirable to behold, and are qualities which in themselves go far to deserve and command national good-fortune. Nor is their pride and confidence exaggerated or unfounded. They possess a country immense in extent and of unparalleled richness. In its virgin soil and limitless prairies are an inexhaustible treasury, a cornucopia from which fatness and abundance for ever flow, while in no part of the world is found such varied mineral wealth. The harvest of field and mine is reaped by an intelligent, industrious, and energetic people, whose territory stretches from ocean to ocean, and this generation will see within its borders one hundred millions of English-speaking people, who will doubtless be prosperous, and who, if they be wise in time, may be also free.

England, who has girdled the earth with empire, and the roots of whose national oak lie, like those

of the mystic tree in Norse sagas, among the
hidden bases of the world, can look without fear,
or distrust, or envy, but rather with a glad and
generous pride, at the development of the great
American people, bone of her bone, and blood of
her blood.   And if England can find nothing
worthy of adoption in the political system of
America, she can yet take care that she does not
fall behind in that noble and confident spirit which
is the birthright of imperial races, and which
enables them to look indifferently on good or evil
fortune.   There are Englishmen who seem to
believe that the golden age has passed for their
country, and that she is falling into decrepitude.
This is not the view of those who have breathed
the free air of the younger and greater Britain in
Canada, Australia, or India.   It is not the spirit
which breathes in Lord Dufferin's Canadian
speeches, or in the admirable address lately delivered by Lord Lorne before the Colonial Institute,
or which inspires the patriotic resolve of Australia
to not only share the glory but the burthens of
the mother-country.   The British Empire is still in
its infancy.   Grafted, it is true, on an ancient
monarchy, it only dates from the occupation of
Virginia by Raleigh three hundred years ago.   It
has grown to be the greatest empire the world has

ever seen, with a territory of 9,000,000 square miles, and 300,000,000 subjects of the Queen, and now only waits the statesman whose genius shall gather it into one mighty federation, animated by loyalty and dignified by freedom. When that day shall come we may hope that the united Anglo-Saxon race, English and American, will join hands across the Atlantic, and, disdaining all possible occasion of quarrel, cement a lasting alliance which will insure the peace and progress of the world.

THE END.

LONDON : R. CLAY, SONS, AND TAYLOR, PRINTERS.

For EU product safety concerns, contact us at Calle de José Abascal, 56–1°,
28003 Madrid, Spain or eugpsr@cambridge.org.

www.ingramcontent.com/pod-product-compliance
Ingram Content Group UK Ltd.
Pitfield, Milton Keynes, MK11 3LW, UK
UKHW012345130625
459647UK00009B/548